SWARTZBURG
BUSSEY

LIBRARIES AND ARCHIVES

PUBLIC LIBRARY BUILDINGS, 1975–1983

MASSIMO & GABRIELLA CARMASSI SENIGALLIA P...

MARC LIBRARY WELARETS

BREISCH
**
*

HENRY

HOBSON

RICHARDSON

AND THE

SMALL

PUBLIC

LIBRARY IN

AMERICA
**
*

University of Pennsylvania Library   Frank Furness

KASER

THE EVOLUTION OF THE AMERICAN ACADEMIC LIBRARY BUILDING

9 788495 951632

ACTAR
V

Phoenix Central Library

bruderDWLarchitects

SB

INTERIOR DESIGN FOR LIBRARIES

Brown

PLANNING AND DESIGNING LIBRARIES FOR CHILDREN AND YOUNG PEOPLE

Michael Dewe

wards

UNIVERSITY LIBRARY BUILDING PLANNING

McCabe
Kennedy

Planning the Modern Public Library Build

Katherina costi regis filia oim q: liberaliii arti
uum studijs erudita et mirabili pulcritudie
omnuii oculis admirablis i alexandria ciui
tate egypti tepore naxeay imperatoris claruit

St. Catherine of Alexandria

"*Meet me at the library.*
Any library.
Every library."

PETER GREENAWAY ~ *The Pillow Book*

LOGOTOPIA
THE LIBRARY IN ARCHITECTURE, ART AND THE IMAGINATION

CURATED BY: SASCHA HASTINGS

Edited by: Sascha Hastings and Esther E. Shipman

With contributions by:

Architects: Hariri Pontarini Architects, Kongats Architects Inc.,
Patkau Architects, Shigeru Ban Architects, Shim-Sutcliffe Architects,
Snøhetta Architects

Artists: Adam David Brown, Douglas Coupland, Denis Farley,
Guy Laramée, Michael Lewis

Writers: Lise Bissonnette, Ray Bradbury, Alberto Manguel,
Robert Jan van Pelt, Nora Young

DIRECTOR'S MESSAGE
MARY MISNER

Cambridge Galleries' Design at Riverside gallery is pleased to present *Logotopia: The Library in Architecture, Art and the Imagination,* curated by Sascha Hastings. As a public art gallery within a public library system, one with a mission to present exhibitions that feature visual art as well as architecture and design, we are in an ideal place to put forward this particular exhibition.

Cambridge Libraries and Galleries' ongoing interest in architecture and commitment to community engagement is clear in the exceptional design of our public buildings and in our 30 year history of presenting contemporary visual art programming.

The opening of our Design at Riverside gallery (2004), located within the University of Waterloo School of Architecture, has given us an even wider mandate to explore the connections between art and architecture and to develop greater public awareness and appreciation for these art forms.

We are grateful for the ongoing support of The City of Cambridge, the Ontario Arts Council and the Canada Council for the Arts and wish to acknowledge the additional support that this exhibition and publication have received from the Canada Council for the Arts through their Promotion of Architecture Program.

Sascha Hastings' curatorial vision for *Logotopia* has been realized through a layering of ideas, information and imagery from diverse sources. Her collaboration with architects, historians, writers and artists has resulted in both an exhibition and a publication that intrigue, inform and provoke discussion. She brings to this project her love of books, her curiosity and a passion for art and architecture, along with a desire to share this enthusiasm with a wider audience.

We thank all of the architectural firms for their kind cooperation and participation. Hariri Pontarini Architects, Kongats Architects Inc., Patkau Architects, Shigeru Ban Architects, Shim-Sutcliffe Architects and Snøhetta Architects have shared their inspirations and their deep appreciation for libraries of all types, in both Canadian and international contexts.

An eclectic roster of writers has generously contributed to the *Logotopia* publication. Their essays inform and expand the dialogue in the curator's multi-disciplinary tribute to the library. We sincerely appreciate the contributions made by Lise Bissonnette, Ray Bradbury, Alberto Manguel, Robert Jan van Pelt and Nora Young.

Our thanks goes to artists Adam David Brown, Douglas Coupland, Denis Farley, Guy Laramée and Michael Lewis for adding yet another dimension to the experience of *Logotopia.* Their works in a wide range of media, chosen for their visual commentary on the notion of the library, create a meaningful link between art, architecture and literature.

The talent of Bhandari & Plater Inc. is evident in the publication and in the exhibition design as well. We thank Laurie Plater for her creativity, resourcefulness and for the guidance she provided throughout the development and realization of this project. As well, the editorial assistance provided by Esther E. Shipman and Marco Polo in the production of the publication is sincerely appreciated.

It is with great pride that we present *Logotopia: The Library in Architecture, Art and the Imagination.* Our most sincere thanks go to the curator, Sascha Hastings, for her vision, dedication and commitment to creating a truly exceptional experience in this exhibition.

Mary Misner, Director
Cambridge Galleries

WORD PLACE
SASCHA HASTINGS

The title of this exhibition, *Logotopia*, comes from the Ancient Greek *logos*, meaning "word", and *topos*, meaning "place". The library is a "word place", the ultimate confluence of language and architecture.

My own experience with word places began in my parents' living room. Built into the wall beneath a bookcase was a small cupboard, its handles low enough that a determined toddler could tug the doors open. Inside lay a treasure trove of children's books – a feast of memorable stories, characters and illustrations to become immersed in for hours on end.

This was followed by the ritual of weekly excursions to the local public library, where crossing the threshold from the busy street into the hushed atmosphere of the main reception area, the intoxicating mixture of scents of books, human bodies and industrial cleaning fluids never failed to stir in me the same frisson of anticipation I get in airports today – the promise of travel to new worlds.

Still later, I discovered my father's book-lined study, with its idiosyncratic collection, and then, the seemingly infinite world within "Fort Book" (nickname for the University of Toronto's Robarts Library, often regarded as a hulking example of Brutalist architecture), where I began roaming the shelves and making random and delightful discoveries. I know that I was not alone in this enterprise. There was a sense of unspoken complicity among the stack seekers, like we were members of a secret society.

Libraries are places where we can be simultaneously alone and part of a community. They are public spaces that allow for private contemplation, where people can spend their time largely as they please and where access to large collections of printed materials, films, music and the Internet is free. Libraries encourage visitors to seek out new information and frequently provide forums for the discussion of books, authors and ideas, or venues for the presentation of music, art, lectures and films.

The *Logotopia* project began with the intriguing notion that given the right combination of factors – engaging architecture, central location, helpful and knowledgeable staff, and strong public programming – a library has the power and the tools to actively and positively affect both individuals and the community as a whole; that a library can reinforce civic pride and breathe life into aging or neglected districts; that the library is as relevant a place today to nurture new ideas and encourage access to a vast knowledge network as it always has been.

As I delved into the idea of the library as an entity, certain recurring themes began to emerge and eventually became the basis for the division of *Logotopia* into spheres of reference – the Universal Library, the National Library, the Public Library, the Private Library and a preliminary investigation of the future of the library, the librarian and the role of new technology.

My research through the real and virtual stacks, and the many ensuing discussions began to reveal the historic impact of the library on a variety of artistic disciplines including architecture, art, film and literature as well as the large body of work that was dedicated to, or that made reference to the influence of the library.

Of particular inspiration to me was the book *Living Library* by Dutch architect Wiel Arets, which documents the creation of the Utrecht University Library from conception to realization. The book is punctuated with interviews, essays (both written and photographic) and references to artforms other than architecture. *Living Library* served as a muse for the development of a multi-disciplinary approach to *Logotopia,* resulting in a publication and exhibition comprised of art, architecture and the written word in almost equal proportions.

The list of contributors is extensive and includes celebrated names as well as emerging voices.

Logotopia invites the reader and the exhibition visitor to immerse themselves in the world of the library, both physical and metaphysical, and to embrace the library in architecture, art and the imagination.

DATE

UNIVERSAL

"Unceasing human work gave birth to this Infinity of books."

JORGE LUIS BORGES ~ *Alexandria, 64 A.D.*

011

THE UNIVERSAL LIBRARY

Detail of grey granite wall,
Bibliotheca Alexandrina

The idea of a universal library has been part of western consciousness since the Ancient Library of Alexandria was founded circa 295 BC. Although we do not know what it looked like – no written descriptions or visual likenesses by its contemporaries exist today – we can be fairly certain that the library was created by King Ptolemy I, a former general of Alexander the Great who became ruler of Egypt after Alexander died. It is believed that Ptolemy collaborated on this monumental task with his advisor, Demetrius of Phaleron, a member of Socrates' famed Peripatetic School and a former Athenian politician and that Ptolemy's son, Ptolemy II Philadelphus, also played a significant role.

The library had a lofty goal: to gather in one place all the knowledge of the world (as it was known to the ancient Greeks), and to create a central hub for research, learning and cultural exchange.

However, the library was probably not a library in today's sense of the word – a discrete building with a central information desk, helpful librarians, open stacks, a reading room and public access. It was most likely incorporated into a larger complex of buildings known as the *Mouseion* or "Temple of the Muses", which stood within the walls of the royal quarter on the edge of the eastern harbour of Alexandria. The *Mouseion* and library were open to writers, scholars and scientists from around the world, but certainly not to the local general public. Its "books" were in fact papyrus and vellum scrolls, both mixed (containing more than one work) and unmixed (containing a single work only), and were probably stored in cupboards, on shelves or in recesses in the walls, in one or more areas of the *Mouseion.* At the height of its fame, the library, and its smaller daughter library, or *Serapeum* ("Temple of Serapis", which had been built to hold overflow from the main library), housed up to 700,000 scrolls containing works of literature, history, theatre, mathematics, geography and science.

The scrolls were acquired in a number of ways – many were purchased abroad. Others were borrowed from libraries throughout the Greek world, copied, and returned to their owners. Still others were seized from ships that docked in Alexandria, where local scholars determined whether to return the books, confiscate them permanently or replace them with copies. In this way, the Ancient Library of Alexandria compiled the most complete collection of ancient learning anywhere.

For all its fame and glory, it seems strange that we know so little about the Ancient Library of Alexandria today, and stranger still that we can't be sure what caused its ultimate demise. Whether by war, fire, looting, natural disaster, neglect or a combination of several events, by the end of the 4th century AD, the Ancient Library of Alexandria had completely ceased to exist as an intellectual or cultural force.

But perhaps the mysteries surrounding this "lost" library are what have made the idea of the universal library endure through the ages, and why it remains such a compelling source of artistic inspiration. This first section of *Logotopia* takes an in-depth look at the new Bibliotheca Alexandrina by the Norwegian firm Snøhetta Architects, including extensive photographs, drawings and an interview with partner Robert Greenwood. Also included here is an essay by Professor Robert Jan van Pelt, tracing the history of the universal library from ancient Alexandria to cyberspace, and illustrated with a wide range of images. Lastly, artist Guy Laramée provides a cheeky take on Jorge Luis Borges' tale *The Library of Babel*.

Hall in the Ancient Library of Alexandria. Woodcut, unsigned, coloured at a later stage

Terraced reading room, Bibliotheca Alexandrina

THE UNIVERSAL LIBRARY
ROBERT JAN VAN PELT

Vincenzo Camuccini, *Ptolemy II Philadelphus founds the Library of Alexandria*. 1813, oil on canvas (top)

The Great Hall of the Ancient Library of Alexandria, from: Carl Sagan, *Cosmos* (bottom)

"At the beginning of the 3ʳᵈ century before our era, a great enterprise was conceived in ancient Alexandria, meeting-place of peoples and cultures: the edification of a Library in the lineage of Aristotle's Lyceum, transposing Alexander's dreams of empire into a quest for universal knowledge." Thus begins the Aswan Declaration, signed in February 1990 by Egyptian President Hosni Mubarak and other dignitaries. The declaration speaks of the wish "to revive the Ancient Library of Alexandria by restating its universal legacy in modern terms," and promises that the new Bibliotheca Alexandrina will be a testimony to "a decisive moment in the history of human thought – the attempt to constitute a summum of knowledge, to assemble the writings of all the peoples." Aiming to encompass "the totality and diversity of human experience," the new library was to become "the matrix for a new spirit of critical inquiry."[1]

Today, a beautiful new library has been built, close to the location of the original and rich in symbolic associations. "Its circular shape, for example, symbolizes the ancient idea of a sphere containing all knowledge," one the architects of the Norwegian firm Snøhetta explained. "Its tilted roof symbolizes the rising sun. It is a beacon of light on the shores of the Mediterranean."[2] The reading room, with space for 1,700 users, is the largest in the world, and its shelf space, with room for eight million books, is said to be the longest in the world.

But the radiance of the Bibliotheca Alexandrina's architecture, its noble intentions and its ancient associations were overshadowed by controversy on its opening day. The library's manuscript centre contributed to the occasion with an exhibition of the holy books of the monotheistic religions. However its display did not only show the Bible and the Torah, but also the first Arabic translation of the notorious Czarist forgery *The Protocols of the Elders of Zion*. According to an article in the Egyptian weekly *al-Usbu'*, the centre's director Youssef Ziedan justified the exhibition of this anti-semitic tract with the explanation that, while not a monotheistic holy book, "it has become one of the sacred [texts] of the Jews, next to their first constitution, their religious law, [and] their way of life. In other words, it is not merely an ideological or theoretical book." Claiming that *The Protocols of the Elders of Zion* "is more important to the Zionist Jews of the world than the Torah," Ziedan was further quoted as saying that it was "only natural to place the book in the framework of an exhibit of Torah." Within days, international outrage drowned out the festive mood in Alexandria. The Director of the Bibliotheca ordered *The Protocols* to be removed from the exhibition, and Ziedan went on record on his website www.ziedan.com that the quotes attributed to him were "fabricated, groundless lies" and that *The Protocols* was "a racist, silly, fabricated book."[3] Yet the damage was done. In an age in which, thanks to the Internet, every small incident can assume global proportions, the hateful *Protocols* became the primary association many had when they thought of the new Bibliotheca Alexandrina, not the cosmopolitan spirit of the Ancient Library of Alexandria or the hope of the library's sponsors and directorate that it would become "a place of dialogue and understanding between cultures and peoples."[4] A further source of embarrassment was the fact that some 90 percent of the shelf space in the new Bibliotheca Alexandrina remained devoid of books, paralleling Gibbon's observation that, after Archbishop Theopilus' purge of non-Christian texts from the Ancient Library of Alexandria, "the appearance of the empty shelves excited the regret and indignation of every spectator, whose mind was not wholly darkened by religious prejudice."[5]

1. http://www.touregypt.net/library/revivald.htm (accessed 25 April 2007).
2. Helena Smith, "Capital of Memory," *The New Statesman* (3 September 2001), 24.
3. www.ziedan.com/English/zion/1.asp
4. http://www.bibalex.org/libraries/presentation/static/15110.aspx (accessed 27 April 2007).
5. Edward Gibbon, *The History of the Decline and Fall of the Roman Empire*, 12 vols. (London: Strahan and Cadell, 1792), vol. 5, 112.

In some way the Bibliotheca Alexandrina's empty shelves and the moral and intellectual controversy on the opening day put a contemporary face on what may be the only enduring legacy of the Ancient Library of Alexandria: its failure to live up to its own idealistic standards. In the final hour of his PBS series *Cosmos* (1980), the late Carl Sagan claimed that science and technology had opened a new horizon of social and economic justice. Such a promise had existed only once before: "It had its citadel at the Library of Alexandria, where 2,000 years ago the best minds of antiquity established the foundations of the systematic study of mathematics, physics, biology, astronomy, literature, geography and medicine."[6] The Alexandria Library contained in its collections of books from all known nations and through the work of its scholars and scientists "the seeds of the modern world." But, according to Sagan, the seeds had never taken root because those involved with the library were not interested in challenging the political, social and economic basis of their society or in the practical application of their discoveries. As a result, "science never captured the imagination of the multitude. There was no counterbalance to stagnation, to pessimism, to the most abject surrenders to mysticism. When, at long last, the mob came to burn the Library down, there was nobody to stop them."[7] For Sagan, the destruction of the library had led to the Dark Ages: "It was as if the entire civilization had undergone some self-inflicted brain surgery, and most of its memories, discoveries, ideas and passions were extinguished irrevocably."[8] In 1980 it looked to many, Sagan included, as though the world faced such a voluntary lobotomy once again as it appeared to be on the brink of surrendering to the inexorable logic that results when ethnic, national and ideological chauvinisms meet the arms race: thermonuclear devastation and the end of all life on earth.

Sagan's decision to foreground the fate of the Alexandria Library in the final program of his series made good use of a collective memory within the West that reads the loss of that library as a symbol of the fragility of civilization. Although nobody knows what ultimately caused the decline and destruction of the library – whether it was a fire set by the troops of Julius Caesar, lawless pillages, well-considered purges, or merely centuries of neglect – one particular legend of the final days of the library had wide currency by the Middle Ages. Upon the Arab conquest of Egypt in 642, Caliph Omar was said to have ordered the destruction of all books that remained in the Alexandria Library with the words "if their contents agree with the Book of God [that is, the Qu'ran], then having the Book of God we are wealthy without them, and if they contradict the Book of God we have no need of them."[9] And thus the remnants of the greatest and richest library in the world were allegedly thrown into the fires that heated the city baths. Much ink has been spilled over the question of whether this legend has a factual core. One recent theory suggests that the tale may in fact have been conceived by the Arab writer Ibn-Al-Qifti as a critical response to the systematic mismanagement of libraries and the selling-off of public book collections in medieval Egypt.[10]

Whatever power the memory of the destruction of the Alexandria Library may have had in debates amongst medieval Muslim scholars, its fate certainly acquired renewed relevance during the Renaissance, as Europe faced the onslaught of the Ottoman Empire and the real possibility of the complete destruction of the cultural heritage of Christendom. In 1526 Turkish troops conquered Budapest and pillaged the Royal Library, one of the largest in Europe. This was a tremendous shock to Renaissance

Fire in the Museum of Alexandria, woodcut, unsigned, coloured at a later stage

6. Carl Sagan, *Cosmos* (New York: Random House, 1980), 333f.
7. Ibid., 335.
8. Ibid., 336.
9. Edward Alexander Parsons, *The Alexandrian Library: Glory of the Hellenic World* (New York: American Elsevier Publishing Company, 1952), 414.
10. James Raven, "Introduction: The Resonances of Loss," in James Raven, *Lost Libraries: The Destruction of Great Book Collections since Antiquity* (Basingstoke and New York: Palgrave Macmillan, 2004), 17f.

Title page of 1966 facsimile of
Conrad Gesner's *Bibliotheca Universalis*

humanists, who believed that the pinnacle of civilization had already been reached by the ancient world, and that all progress consisted in reconstructing the knowledge of the Greeks and Romans. Because the primary access to that lost universe was through its texts, libraries where those ancient Greek and Latin works were collected, studied, edited and made ready for re-publication had become the core of western civilization. As such, they needed to be protected.

Anticipating further Turkish victories the Swiss humanist Conrad Gesner decided to construct a sort of literary ark. A scholar without access to wealth or power, he realized he could not physically bring together all of ancient Greek, Roman and Hebrew literature in a safe place. Therefore Gesner decided to create a comprehensive bibliography, which he entitled *Bibliotheca Universalis* (1545). Gesner's 1,264 folio "universal library" listed in its first edition some 3,000 authors and 10,000 books. This virtual library had three aims. First of all, the *Bibliotheca Universalis* gave scholars and rulers a tool to build repositories of the intellectual inheritance of the West out of harm's way in many different and faraway places. Christianity had survived the Dark Ages in Ireland; if the Turks succeeded in Europe, might Iceland or the New World not offer a similar refuge? Secondly, if Christendom collapsed, and all libraries were destroyed, a single copy of the *Bibliotheca Universalis* would allow survivors to realize what they had lost, which might at least trigger a desire to recover it. Finally, the *Bibliotheca Universalis* would counter an inner threat which Gesner believed to be as dangerous as the Turkish army – the chaos that resulted from the unmanageable avalanche of books that a mere century after the invention of the printing press threatened to overwhelm readers. Therefore Gesner provided within the *Bibliotheca Universalis* a knowledge hierarchy that could serve as a blueprint for establishing any library – small or universal. Entitled *Pandectae* or "all-embracing," this was a systematic organization of all knowledge in 20 principal groups, subdivided into secondary groups, then parts and finally segments. A massive matrix to organize the bibliographic universe, the *Pandectae* encompassed 30,000 different concepts.[11]

Unfortunately, the 17th century had neither the resources nor the inclination to realize Gesner's concept. A print from 1614 reveals the library of Leiden University, one of the most famous places of learning in that time, to have been a rather small place.[12] It holds only 22 book presses equipped with lecterns plus one additional closed cabinet that held the valuable collection of 208 books and manuscripts in Hebrew, Arab, Syriac and Ethiopian languages bequeathed to the university by the famous French humanist Joseph Justus Scaliger. Considered the greatest polymath of his times and the author of "a flood of massive, interminable, magnificently unreadable books,"[13] Scaliger had been wooed to Leiden in 1593 by a professorship that did not require teaching and, as Scaliger recalled a decade later, by "the great advantage of the Library."[14] With less than 1,500 volumes, it obviously sufficed; the library offered an enclosed universe that allowed Scaliger and other scholars to engage in comfort the limited number of classical sources that were crucial to the humanistic enterprise. And if someone asked for more, there was always Seneca's rhetorical question "what is the use of having countless books and libraries, whose titles their owners can scarcely read through in a whole lifetime? The learner is not instructed, but burdened by a mass of them, and it is much better to surrender yourself to a few authors than to wander through many."[15]

11. Urs B. Leu, *Conrad Gesner als Theologe: Ein Beitrag zur Zürcher Geistesgeschichte des 16. Jahrhunderts* (Bern: Peter Lang, 1990), 105ff.; Helmut Zedelmaier, *Bibliotheca Universalis und Bibliotheca Selecta: Das Problem der Ordnung des gelehrten Wissens in der frühen Neuzeit* (Cologne, Weimar and Vienna: Böhlau, 1992).

12. The engraving was published in Johannes van Meurs, *Illustrum Hollandiae & Westfrisiae ordinum alma Academiae Leidensis* (Leiden: Jacobus Marcus and Justus à Colster, 1614), 228; the larger and more detailed original was based on a drawing by Jan Cornelisz van 't Woudt and engraved by Willem Isaaksz Swanenburgh in 1609.

13. Anthony Grafton, *Athenae Batavae: The Research Imperative at Leiden*, 1575-1650 (Leiden: Primavera Press, 2003), 22.

14. George W. Robinson, ed., *Autobiography of Joseph Scaliger* (Cambridge: Harvard University Press, 1927), 49.

15. Seneca, *Moral Essays*, John W. Basore trans., 3 vols. (London and New York: Heinemann/G.P Putnam's Sons, 1932), vol. 2, 247ff.

Library of Leiden University. 1614, copper engraving

Herzog August Library Wolfenbüttel, exterior of rotunda. L. Tacke, 1888, oil on canvas

Herzog August Library Wolfenbüttel, interior of rotunda.
L. Tacke, 1888, oil on canvas

Furthermore, librarians were convinced it was their duty to protect the immature reader from temptation. In the early 17th century many believed that a library could be a dangerous place, and either purged collections or locked up "bad books" written by heretics or on non-Christian subjects such as cabala and magic in "poison cabinets". The French librarian Gabriel Naudé, however, didn't agree with this extreme approach. In his *Avis pour dresser une bibliothèque* (1627) Naudé wrote that every library should be universal in scope, "since it may be laid down as a maxim that there is no book whatsoever, be it never so bad or disparaged, but may in time be sought for by someone."[16] Even dangerous texts should be made available, "considered among the rest of the volumes in the library like serpents and vipers among other living creatures, like tares in good wheat, like thorns among roses."[17]

Naudé himself did not take responsibility for the fate of those seduced by the serpents in the stacks, but any librarian who could not pass over the amoral dimensions of a universal library so lightly could always turn to another work on the subject, the *Bibliotheca Selecta* (1593), published by the Italian Jesuit Antonio Possevino. Written in response to Gesner's work, Possevino's "selected library" was conceived as a guide to help the reader navigate the swamps and pitfalls of a large if not universal library. Like Gesner and Naudé, Possevino did not believe in purges or restricting access to "bad books." Instead, believing that reading and the acquisition of knowledge are essential aspects of human life, Possevino focused on the question of how to create a mature reader who would confront the dangers of the universal library, and face them down.[18]

By the late 17th century the importance of the library as a citadel of civilizations and a battleground of ideas began to wane and the promise of the universal library became less relevant. The scientific revolution shifted the paradigm from book-based erudition to research. The challenge against the concept of a universal library was explicitly raised by a man who was not only a great polymath and philosopher, but also a librarian who is remembered as the founder of Library Science. Gottfried Wilhelm Leibniz argued that the key to knowing what was relevant was no longer a mass of books, but asking the correct question and applying the correct method – what he called the "Algebra of Thought" – to one's reasonings.[19] As a result, he suggested that a three- or four-room library would provide all knowledge necessary. At the same time, as steward of the famous Ducal Library in Wolfenbüttel, Leibniz knew that his own career depended on giving his patron a very visible return for his investment, and so he oversaw the construction of the magnificent Baroque building (1706-10). With its central, oval hall derived from church architecture, the library suggested that the Wolfenbüttel collection of 100,000 books was indeed of a universal scope, worthy of a great man such as the Duke, and worthy of a substantial raise for his chief librarian.

Other remarkable libraries were built in 18th century Germany and Austria where quasi-enlightened Abbots of the ancient monastic orders and quasi-sovereign Princes of the Holy Roman Empire – which, in the words of Voltaire, was neither Holy, nor Roman, nor an Empire – competed in commissioning the most beautiful ensembles of books, painting, sculpture, decorative arts and architecture. Paradisal libraries such as Johann Bernhard Fischer von Erlach's Vienna Hofbibliothek (1722-26) or Christian Wiedemann's Wiblingen Abbey (1737-50) suggested that the more spiritual idea of the Universal Library was still alive and well –

16. Gabriel Naudé, *Advice on Establishing a Library* (Berkeley and Los Angeles: University of California Press, 1950), 17.
17. Ibid., 26.
18. Helmut Zedelmaier, *Bibliotheca Universalis und Bibliotheca Selecta: Das Problem der Ordnung des gelehrten Wissens in der frühen Neuzeit* (Cologne, Weimar and Vienna: Böhlau, 1992), 125ff.
19. "Einrichtung einer Bibliothek," in Gottfried Wilhelm Leibniz, *Sämtliche Schriften und Briefe*, Fourth Series, volume three (Berlin: Akademie Verlag, 1986), 350.

Werther reading the *Iliad*. Steel engraving

that despite the catastrophe of the Thirty Years War and despite the new philosophies and discoveries that threatened longstanding traditions, conventions and hierarchies, the chaos could still be tamed into a configuration of significance.

In reality, however, these beautiful spaces were the valedictory speeches for an idea and maybe even an institution that to so many had outlived its use. By the time the last of these great libraries was constructed, the Hall of Philosophers in the Sarov Monastery in Prague (1782-85), to all but its owners libraries had become symbols of an obsolete, dusty world, at best the eccentric lair of bookish pedants and bibliomanes, and at worst the hateful symbols of a hierarchical world in which knowledge was a tool to preserve the social and political status quo. In the so-called Age of Enlightenment, libraries were not yet, as they were to become a hundred years later, public institutions accessible to all, and the *philosophes* who dreamt of new and better societies had little use for them. A quick survey of the utopian literature of the 18th century reveals not a single example of a society that counts a universal library or even a *Grande Bibliothèque* amongst its institutions. For example, in Louis-Sébastien Mercier's *L'An 2440* (1771), the French Royal Library has been reduced to "one small closet." Mercier's fictional librarian explains that the Parisians of the future have realized that "a numerous library was the feat of the greatest extravagancies and the most idle chimeras" and that within those "labyrinths of books" the sciences were "in a perpetual circulation, returning incessantly to the same point," causing men to become "servile imitators, destitute of invention and originality." Hence they had gathered together all the books that were judged "either frivolous, useless, or dangerous" (which was most of them), assembled them in a pyramid that resembled "another Babel," and set fire to it. The librarian was proud of their "enlightened zeal", so different from what the barbarians had done in ignorance: "As we are neither unjust, nor like the Sarrazins, who heated the baths with the chef d'oeuvres of literature, we have made an election; those of the greatest judgment amongst us have extracted the substance of thousands of volumes, which they have included in a small duodecimo; not unlike those skillful chemists, who concenter the virtues of many plants in a small phial, and cast aside the refuse."[20]

Although Mercier allowed a few books, many enlightenment utopias knew only of a single book, *the* book – an idea with deep roots in the more puritan sections of Christian and Muslim communities. In his proto-communist epic poem *Basiliad* (1753), the shadowy writer Étienne-Gabriel Morelly allowed on his island paradise one book which every inhabitant needs to own and know. It begins with a paean to the ruling prince and his wise government, and for the rest provides useful information to negotiate the practicalities of everyday life.[21]

Morelly's idea of the single book had a real future, but very different from what he had imagined. With the advent of the Romantic literary movement, the passions of the heart claimed precedence over the reasonings of the mind, and with that the young, who were supposed to be in closer touch with their feelings, claimed superiority over the old. One was to follow the impulses of nature, and not obey the constraints of civilization. If in the Middle Ages the barbarians at the gate had been "the Sarrazins," and in the 16th century the Turks, now they were the adolescents who challenged the establishment – which meant the whole adult world with all its trappings and treasures, including libraries.

http://www.gutenberg.org

20. Louis Sébastien *Mercier, Memoirs of the Year Two Thousand Five Hundred*, W. Hooper trans., 2 vols. (London: G. Robinson, 1772), vol. 2, 2ff.; see also Raymond Trousson, "Les bibliothèques de l'utopie au XVIIIe siècle," in *Buch und Sammler: Private und öffentliche Bibliotheken im 18. Jahrhundert* (Heidelberg: Carl Winter, 1979), 99-107.
21. Étienne-Gabriel Morelly, *Naufrage des Isles flottantes, ou Basiliade de célèbre Pilpaï*, 2 vols. (Paris: Société de Libraries, 1753), vol. 2, 207f.

Jean-Jacques Rousseau, the self-appointed leader of the revolt of the young, fulminated against books. "I hate books; they only teach us to talk about things we know nothing about," he wrote in *L'Émile* (1760). Yet Rousseau did recognize one book that was useful to educate youngsters such as Emile according to nature: *Robinson Crusoe* – a book about a man who built civilization without the help of books. "This is the first book Emile will read; for a long time it will form his whole library, and it will always retain an honoured place… It will serve to test our progress toward right judgment, and it will always be read with delight, so long as our taste is unspoilt."[22]

However, the charter text of the Romantic movement, the single book about a bookless world that would destroy the relevance of libraries, was Johann Wolfgang Goethe's epistolary novel *The Sorrows of Young Werther*. Like Caliph Omar and Emile, Werther only needs one book, but where the Caliph had the Qu'ran and Emile had *Robinson Crusoe,* Werther carries a pocket edition of Homer's *Iliad* everywhere he goes. Before long, a *Werther* craze swept through Europe, and Goethe's novel became the cult book so many other young men took with them into nature. Such a case is described in Karl Philipp Moritz's autobiographical novel *Anton Reiser*. Young Anton suffers an unhealthy childhood framed by books. But as he grows up, he begins to enjoy nature, and discovers *The Sorrows of Young Werther*. Reiser soon recognizes himself in Werther and treats the book as if had been written just for him. "'Take the little book for your friend, if through fate or your own fault you cannot find one nearer.' These were the words he thought of, whenever he drew the book from his pocket." And thus, "almost every day when the weather was fine with *Werther* in his pocket he went for the river-side walk in the meadow, where the single trees stood, to the little copse, where he was so much at home."[23] And there he reread the book over and over.

The Romantic cult of youth became dominant once again in the second half of the 20th century, and with it revived the cult of the single book that makes even the largest library irrelevant. Jack Kerouac's *On the Road* (1957) proved crucial in shaping the Beat generation, and *The Quotations from Chairman Mao ZeDong* (1964) became the symbol of the frenzied idealism of a revolutionary youth running amok against the structures of the old. Today the Sony Corporation offers a new and highly de-politicized version of the book that will set us free – free from the weight and bulk of libraries, free to embrace the minimalist, transparent and bookless aesthetics popularized in *Dwell, Azure* and *Wallpaper* lifestyle magazines. "As small as a paperback," the Sony®Reader promises with the help of Ink®Technology an "almost paper-like" display that approximates the readability of the printed page.[24] Downloading content from the online Connect™eBookstore, this oversized iPod for readers collapses the distinction between the library and the book. Despite the obvious drawback that it needs, amongst other things, electrical power, the infrastructure of the Internet, a credit card and the continuing existence of the Sony Corporation, the possibilities appear endless when Sony's Connect™eBookstore links up with Google's Project Gutenberg and Carnegie Mellon's Universal Library. Yet even then the perfect synthesis of the universal library and the single book appears bound to be another Tower of Babel in the making. The Carnegie Mellon people may have defined the ultimate aim of their Universal Library "to capture all books in digital format," but they also admit "it is believed that such a task is impossible and could take hundreds of years, and never be completed."[25]

http://www.cmu.edu

22. Jean-Jacques Rousseau, *Emile*, Barbara Foxley trans. (London: J.M. Dent, 1993), 176; see also Heinz Schlaffer, "Die Verachtung der Bücher und die Verehrung des Buches," in Rebekka Habermas and Walter H. Pehle, eds., *Der Autor, der nicht schreibt: Versuche über den Büchermacher und das Buch* (Frankfurt am Main: Fischer, 1989), 18-27.
23. Karl Philipp Moritz, *Anton Reiser*, P. E. Matheson trans. (London: Oxford University Press, 1926), 263f.
24. http://www.learningcenter.sony.us/assets/itpd/reader/reader_features.html (accessed 29 April 2007).
25. http://www.ul.cs.cmu.edu/html/goals.html (accessed 29 April 2007).

Erik Desmazières, *La Bibliothèque de Babel.* 1997, print from First Suite of ten etchings on blue-toned laid paper, edition of 25.°Erik Desmazières/SODRAC (1997)

It is an interesting commentary on our time that today's generation begins to build its assault on the heavens knowing it cannot be done. And probably it ought not to be done. The Argentinian poet, storyteller and librarian Jorge Luis Borges probably saw things correctly when he resurrected Gesner's dream in his nightmarish tale *Bibliotheka de Babel* (1939). Borges' library contains not only all the books that have ever been written, but also that can be written, and has thus become an endless labyrinth. As an imagined, self-evident reality, it touches, extends and finally crushes the reader's imagination. "The universe (which others call the library) is composed of an indefinite, perhaps infinite number of hexagonal galleries... Twenty bookshelves, five to each side, line four of the hexagon's six sides; the height of the bookshelves, floor to ceiling, is hardly greater than the height of a normal librarian. One of the hexagon's free sides opens to a narrow sort of vestibule, which in turn opens onto another gallery, identical to the first – identical in fact to all. To the left and right of the vestibule are two tiny compartments. One is for sleeping, upright, the other, for satisfying one's physical necessities."[26] Borges relates that when, five hundred years ago, a librarian deduced that the library contained all books, people were delighted as they believed that somewhere in the library answers could be found to all questions. "The universe was justified; the universe suddenly became congruent with the unlimited width and breadth of humankind's hopes."[27] But there were no bibliographies, catalogues or shelf lists to point the way to the right hexagon, or the right shelf, and no Possevino to teach the potential user how to orient oneself in the maze. And so hope turned into despair, and the institution that was to provide a beacon of light turned out to be a pit of darkness – hell as it must be imagined in our information age. But as Borges observed in a later comment on the *Bibliotheka de Babel,* human beings like to imagine the horrors and torments of hell. Therefore he had given his readers "the vast, contradictory Library, whose vertical wildernesses of books run the incessant risk of changing into others that affirm, deny, and confuse everything like a delirious god."[28]

As I wander daily through the maze of the Internet in search of provisional answers to ill-defined questions, I often remember Borges' melancholy dream. For all my hope that the largest reading room in the world will indeed increase mutual understanding to a region plagued by hatred, for all my appreciation of the offerings of the Gutenberg Project and Carnegie Mellon's Universal Library, for all my love of the Musagetes Architectural Library in Cambridge, the Sterling Memorial Library in New Haven and the Warburg Library in London as my personal places of discovery, I sense that we are all now chained to the World Wide Web like Borges' readers to their hexagons, a fate so well depicted in Erik Desmazières' recent engravings of Borges' gigantic but at the same time claustrophobic library.[29] It must give food for thought that the closest approximation of Giovanni Battista Piranesi's dystopian vision embodied in his *Carceri* has a universal library as its contemporary locus and topos. And even if some student will occasionally escape from her desk to wander to a wireless-less spot with her Sony®Reader, taking in the individually selected, uploaded and managed "content," I doubt she will ever be able to rediscover the unique pleasure that comes with the discovery of a dusty, somewhat tatty book in a musty corner of a real-life library that, despite its earlier history, appears to have been written, printed, bound, bought, registered, stamped, shelved and preserved just for her.

26. Jorge Luis Borges, "The Library of Babel," in Jorge Luis Borges, *Collected Fictions*, Andrew Hurley trans. (New York: Viking, 1998), 112.

27. Ibid., 115.

28. Jorge Luis Borges, "The Total Library," in Jorge Luis Borges, *Selected Non-Fictions*, Eliot Weinberger ed. (New York: Viking, 1999), 216.

29. These engravings are published in Jorge Luis Borges, *The Library of Babel*, Andrew Hurley trans., Erik Desmazières ill. (Boston: David R. Godine, 2000).

BIBLIOTHECA ALEXANDRINA
SNØHETTA ARCHITECTS

Alexandria, Egypt
Completed 2002

An interview between Sascha Hastings (SH) and Robert Greenwood (RG)

Plan of Harbour of Alexandria, Egypt.
Location of Bibliotheca Alexandrina is marked with a red dot

When Snøhetta Architects won the international competition to design a new Library of Alexandria in 1989, none were more surprised than the young and still practically unknown Norwegian architecture firm, whose oldest member was a mere 33 at the time. Thirteen years later, the beautiful new library, with its iconic, sliced cylindrical design, sits in the harbour of the city founded by Alexander the Great in 331 BC and close to the presumed site of the legendary Ancient Library of Alexandria. The new library, or Bibliotheca Alexandrina, was an overnight architectural success, and launched the career of Snøhetta, which now designs major projects all over the world. Curator Sascha Hastings spoke to Robert Greenwood, a partner at Snøhetta Architects, from his office in Oslo, Norway.

SH: In what ways did the Ancient Library of Alexandria influence the Bibliotheca Alexandrina?

RG: I think different people would answer this in different ways, but I would say not at all, except that the place, Alexandria, is an important part of our collective history. The actual library that was there more than 2,000 years ago wasn't a theme for us at all, because nobody knows what it looked like, and it was probably a whole collection of buildings, not a library as we understand it today. So I think the only importance of the ancient library was its mythical and historical place in our culture.

SH: Let's talk about the design. What are the library's most important features?

RG: The most important feature is the section through the library. This sloping line breaks the horizontal of the ground and goes under the earth, referring to history and the past, and then rises up to the sky, referring to the future. So the idea that you can have both the future and the past in this building is important.

SH: You've also punched skylights into the sloped roof...

RG: Yes. We always had the idea – the rather romantic idea – that you could sit in the library and look out across the sea. In this way, the reading room becomes an actual landscape – just like a terraced hillside – and so you can sit on one of the terraces and be on the same height as the sea and look out across the ocean, out, in fact, back towards Greece.

SH: The circle and volumes derived from the circle play a big part in the library's design. Can you tell me more about this?

RG: It's quite interesting about the building's geometry. We designed the library back in the days when computers were still in their infancy, so it was drawn with pens and pencils. You can put a compass in the middle and draw the plan, so the geometry is an ellipse at an angle to the ground, and when you cut it, you get circles. It's also a reference to the harbour, which is circular in shape and an absolutely beautiful site for the building.

The Bibliotheca Alexandrina at night

SH: The curved exterior wall is clad in granite panels with letters and characters chiseled into them. What's the significance?
RG: The wall is the big decorative element. The intention was that on the surface of the wall you could find every written character from the history of humankind – Arabic script, Roman letters, even Braille – so it's a collection of graphics that reflects the history of writing. But there are no actual words – you can't read anything – you can only appreciate the graphics.

The stone on the wall is all from Egypt. We went through a long process to find the right stone and had to open a new quarry in the south. It's a grey granite, quarried in a special way to get the natural finish of the stone – so it's not sawn, rather it's split out of the rock using wedges. It has to be done by skilled quarriers, because they have to be able to read the rock and know which direction it's going to split out, so in many ways it's a technology that Alexander himself would have appreciated. The stones are about a metre thick and they vary in size – there are a couple of modules, but the biggest are two metres by about a metre wide. And after they were quarried they were all carved by hand in Alexandria – people sitting down on the ground with a full-sized template and chiseling it out.

SH: What was it like for local people to build their own library?
RG: There's a huge amount of local pride in the building. Particularly the quarriers and stonemasons had an amazing sense of history in what they were doing. In fact, because many of the skills had been lost, we took them up to Norway to different quarries to give them a bit of guidance. It's quite a fantastic achievement – about 5,000 square metres of hand carved granite.

SH: What was the biggest challenge in building this library?
RG: Just building it at all! At many points in the process, and it was a long process, we said "Well, this looks like it really isn't going to happen", mainly because of money and politics. It was also quite an unlikely event to achieve a building of this quality in Alexandria at that time, since there were not very many buildings of that quality in Egypt then. They're coming now, for example, the new museum they're building in Cairo, but I think the library set a precedent, not only among architects there, but also among contractors.

SH: Getting back to the Ancient Library of Alexandria, the idea of a universal library has been around for almost 2,500 years. How relevant do you think this idea is today?
RG: I don't think that the library in Alexandria as it now stands is really a universal library – it's not being run in the same way as the original library was when they were trying to gather everything. A lot of people have also questioned whether a library is of any relevance in a country where half the people are illiterate, but I think that the library in Alexandria is playing a huge role in the culture and particularly among young people. It's very interesting to be there – it's very popular – you can see it when you're standing in line to get in. The library now is not so much a storehouse of knowledge as a place where people can meet.

Detail of grey granite wall, inscribed with different characters and alphabets

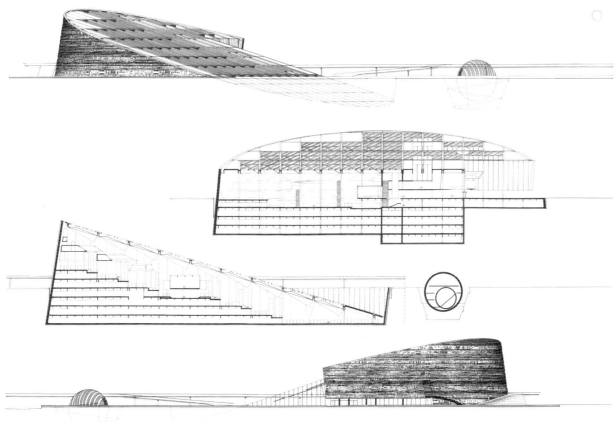

Elevation and section drawings of the Bibliotheca Alexandrina

And that is very relevant and also a way of exchanging information. And it's working on different levels – you have the Internet and all these possibilities. I mean, you could stay home and read every book in the world, but the interesting thing about the library is that it brings the analogue and the digital worlds together, and you can mix those two. I think

at this stage, that's a very important thing in our culture.

SH: One of the Bibliotheca Alexandrina's stated goals is to promote international peace and understanding. Isn't that a tall order for a library?

RG: It is a tall order, but you have to think of it more as an institution than a physical building. A building itself doesn't just do that – you need

the people behind it. I also think time is very important because the build-up to an institution like this takes a generation or more – many generations probably. Alexandria has an interesting history – if you go back a couple of generations it was a very multicultural centre, taking in all the cultures of the Mediterranean. That all stopped around the 1940s and '50s.

Maybe now they have a chance to regain that position, where Alexandria once again can become an intellectual centre on the Mediterranean.

View down into terraced reading room

View across landscaped terrace and skylights of reading room

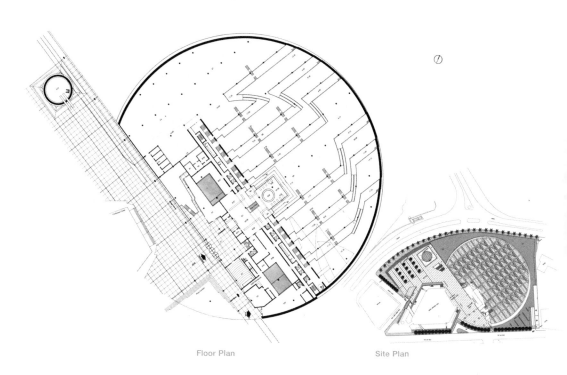

Floor Plan

Site Plan

Aerial view of the Bibliotheca Alexandrina with the city of Alexandria stretching out behind

BORGES' LAST COFFEE

GUY LARAMÉE

Montréal, 2006

Borges' health was rapidly declining, and against his doctors' advice, he decided to have a coffee, just the way he used to do at the Cafe del Tiempo on Paseo de la Reforma in Buenos Aires.

Because of his heart condition, he had not swallowed a drop of caffeine in months. The moment the coffee touched his lips he was launched into the most extravagant visual hallucination (he had been blind for the past 15 years, but this had never impaired his inner vision). To secure this vision, he took a second sip. In a moment he was right back in the corridors of his library, the Library of Babel, of course, exactly the way he had seen it when he first wrote the story. But now, there was a difference: the library was collapsing. Or was it really a collapse? It was hard to tell, because where the library was once made up of identical hexagonal galleries, it now seemed to have developed a spiral shape. It seemed to be twisting,

turning, suffering, utterly suffering. It seemed to be possessed by a tremendous struggle (the struggle between order and chaos perhaps?); it looked like it was recoiling out of pain. "That's it!" thought Borges, "The Universal Library suffers the Universal Pain: it suffers the pain of Knowledge!" Digging further into his vision he saw the library starting to climb to the sky, organically, as if it were made of vapours dissipating into the air. He looked down: the library was growing out of his own coffee mug! Could it be that simple? All these years, all this writing, could it have been caused by his addiction to coffee? He could not reach his cup for the last sip; his heart gave up under the weight of this revelation.

Guy Laramée, *Borges' Last Coffee.* 2006, basswood, table with metal stand, chair

NATIONAL

*"When any nation
starts awake
Books are the memory."*

TED HUGHES ~ *Hear it Again*

THE NATIONAL LIBRARY

Illustration of British Library Reading Room by Sidney Smirke, *Illustrated London News*, 1857

Next to the national parliament, the national library is arguably a country's most important civic building. It is responsible for the collection and preservation of the cultural heritage of the nation – all the books, manuscripts, images and other materials that relate to its history. As such, it is a storehouse of national memory, a political symbol and an embodiment of how a nation sees itself and wishes to be perceived by others. Thanks to the so-called right of deposit, at least one copy of every book, periodical and other copyrighted material must be given to most national libraries by law.

National libraries also contain rare or unique documents and therefore need to place strict conditions on how their collections are made available to the public. Architecturally, the scholarly research nature of national libraries has informed the tradition of the grand reading room, which is both an expression of the collective knowledge of the nation and a guarantee of visibility and security. Sidney Smirke's great domed reading room designed for the British Library (1852), with staff at the centre of a radiating system of bookcases and reading areas, influenced library design for decades.

Many of the great national libraries of the world began in whole or in part as the private libraries of royalty, wealthy individuals or both. For example, the National Library of France or Bibliothèque nationale de France (BnF) had its beginnings as early as the 14th century in the royal library, which accompanied the King and his court in their peregrinations from palace to castle to country house, until it became so big that Louis XIV gave it a permanent home in central Paris. The collection continued to grow, particularly during and after the French Revolution, when it amalgamated libraries confiscated from the nobility and the Church into its collection. By the middle of the 19th century, the library had grown so large, and the task of expanding its premises so immense, that architect Henri Labrouste required six years to complete it. Labrouste's lasting legacy was his famous Salle Labrouste reading room (1862), with its glazed vaults and innovative cast iron structure.

More than a century later, the BnF needed to expand again. In 1989, Dominique Perrault Architecte won the competition to build the new Bibliothèque nationale de France François Mitterand on a former industrial site in eastern Paris, where the library was a key part of a broader urban renewal plan. This library is now one of the most significant in the world, and an architectural icon in France.

Inspired in part by the example of the BnF, the National Library and Archives of Québec or Bibliothèque et Archives nationales du Québec (BAnQ) decided to build a new central library in Montréal (2005). The library's visionary President and Chief Executive Officer, Lise Bissonnette, recounts that undertaking in the next few pages. Then we take a trip through the BAnQ's new Grande Bibliothèque, designed by Patkau Architects in association with Croft Pelletier and Menkès Shooner Dagenais Architectes Associées, followed by photographs by artist Denis Farley that were inspired in part by the new national libraries in Montréal and Paris. Finally, we share a blog excerpt by Dr. Saad Eskander, the Director of the Iraq National Library and Archive in Baghdad, about what it's like to run a national library during a time of occupation and civil war.

The Salle Labrouste reading room, National Library of France

Bibliothèque nationale de France François Mitterand

A SPACE OF FREEDOM
LISE BISSONNETTE

Staircase at heart of General Collection

Sometimes, the magic works. Sometimes the dream emerges from the most demanding of rational processes, as the recent genesis of the Grande Bibliothèque du Québec, inaugurated in spring 2005 in Montréal, shows.

It all began in the 1960s. The dynamism of Québec's public libraries went hand in hand with a growing awareness that the means at their disposal fell short of increasing public expectations. The lack of space and the need to rapidly adapt to the new technologies led government authorities to launch an in-depth reflection on the problem. But it was a long, chaotic road that would finally lead from the critical situation the Bibliothèque centrale de Montréal faced in the 1980s to the creation of its successor institution, the Grande Bibliothèque du Québec, in 1998.

The challenge was great, because the new institution had a particularly ambitious mission. It was to "be an engine for intellectual life in Québec; provide democratic access to a national and universal collection of great quality; focus on the dissemination of knowledge and information; have a positive, stimulating effect on all Québec libraries; and promote exemplary use of the new technologies" (*Rapport. Une grande bibliothèque pour le Québec,* Gouvernement du Québec, 1997, p. 44).

Here already, we get an inkling of the originality and drawing power of an institution whose astounding development over the next ten years no one then suspected.

What was clear, from that moment, was that the project demanded a vast, welcoming, easily accessible space fully integrating the latest technological innovations.

Early in 2000 an international architectural competition was launched. The call for expressions of interest, open for six months, brought in 37 proposals, five of which were short-listed. During a second stage, the five finalists prepared their design concepts for evaluation by the jury. As a first indication that this was no ordinary project, the proposals of the finalists were outstanding and inspired, and the choice was difficult for the distinguished panel chaired by Phyllis Lambert. Ultimately, the winning submission was the one presented by Patkau Architects of Vancouver, in association with two firms from Québec City: Croft Pelletier and Gilles Guité. In 2002, a third team – Menkès Shooner Dagenais – was placed in charge of project realization, preparation of working drawings and construction site supervision.

Through the merging of these talents, a superb, multifaceted building issued forth, with unmistakably unique characteristics.

The first of these is space, or rather spaces, because different areas representative of the missions of the institution are connected by functional, elegant circulation systems. For visitors in a hurry, there is the rapid ascent and descent of glass elevators. Users on a quest of discovery can keep a constant eye on the collections, within easy reach at switchback turns in a suspended stairway of striking esthetic quality. For readers seeking comfort and serenity, an architectural promenade lazily winds along the walls of the building, with peaceful little way stations for study and reflection.

Next are the materials. Glass, concrete and wood blend harmoniously in the Grande Bibliothèque, providing not only light, transparency and sobriety, but warmth and comfort as well. The same elements that are essential to the building's structure recur in the magnificent furniture designed by Michel Dallaire to make users feel at home. Emblematic of the Québec

Grande Bibliothèque du Québec at night

Main entrance on rue Berri

Reading room and promenade between General Collection (left) and National Collection (right)

touch in the project, two wooden rooms inspired by Anne Hébert's famous novel *Les Chambres de bois (The Silent Rooms),* published in 1958, provide an amber-hued enclosure for the library's collections. Here too, light filters through the yellow birch slats of the louvred walls, gently bathing the premises.

Finally, there is the dialogue with the city. The Grande Bibliothèque seems, indeed, a model of urban integration. The choice of location, in the heart of Montréal's Latin Quarter, where a university, theatres, restaurants and trendy businesses rub elbows, puts it in direct touch with one of the most dynamic areas in town, to which people stream on the city's main Metro lines or via the central bus station serving all of Québec and numerous destinations in the United States. This urban foothold is strengthened further by the fluid connection between the building's interior circulation routes and the main thoroughfares bordering the building, naturally extending them east to west and north to south. From everywhere, the city draws in to the library, which, in turn, reaches out to the city and beautifully transitions into it through gardens and artworks.

It is a winning combination: a challenge conquered, in terms of the objectives set by the initiators of the project; premises perfectly suited to the problem at hand. And success was not long in coming. In its first two years of existence, the Grande Bibliothèque has attracted five million visitors, far exceeding the most optimistic predictions. Nearly 10,000 people come here on any given day. Their movement is fascinating, in both its scope and complexity. Their paths cross in a continuous ballet – scholars and adult literacy learners, babies and seniors, rich and less well off, middle-classers and punkers – late into the night.

No doubt, the success confirms the appropriateness and quality of the architectural choices made, as well as the suitability of the documents and services provided to the public by an enthusiastic and devoted staff. But these accomplishments, no matter how great, are only outward signs. For the fact that so many people have made themselves at home here points to an intangible, but essential dimension of the Grande Bibliothèque, which, in its urban environment, has become a place of free expression, respect and dialogue like no other, a place for community life, where social ties, constantly imperilled in major cities, are recreated moment by moment.

Where else, indeed, do people find free access to knowledge and culture without having to answer for their intellectual or social status? Where else can they advance their learning guided by their own choices, unencumbered by laws or market conditioning?

The creation of the Grande Bibliothèque turned on its ear a Québec documentary landscape long content with the traditional, reassuring schemes adopted by countless libraries in the world up until the end of the 20th century. It stimulated in-depth thinking, disruptive and fruitful enough to provoke the birth of an institution unique in the world today – Bibliothèque et Archives nationales du Québec – integrating the missions of a national library, national archives, a major public library and a true virtual library.

Some people, apparently, find the idea of continuing to build large public libraries most incongruous in this day of the Internet, which they say will soon turn them into deserted, useless places. But that is to completely misunderstand the emergence of the new role, precious among all others, of an institution more indispensable than ever in city centres as the ultimate space of humanity and freedom.

Reading room inside National Collection (top)

View into public concourse and General Collection, with reading spaces at perimeter (bottom)

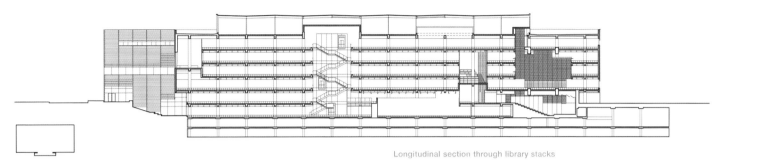

Longitudinal section through library stacks

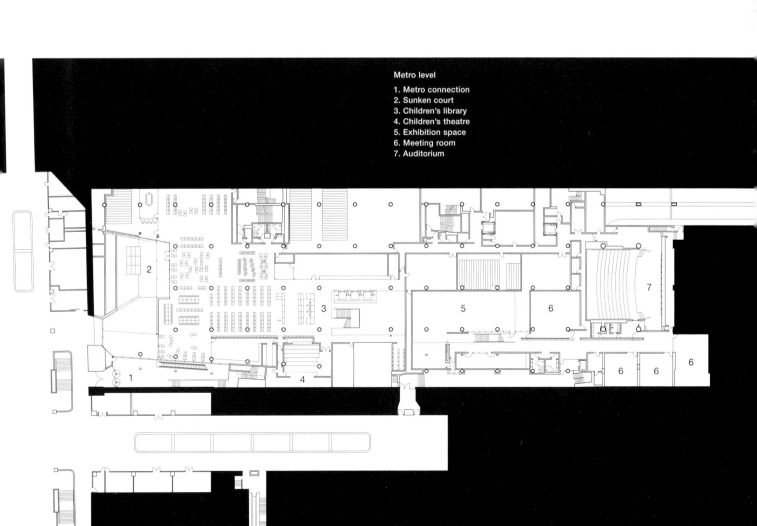

Metro level

1. Metro connection
2. Sunken court
3. Children's library
4. Children's theatre
5. Exhibition space
6. Meeting room
7. Auditorium

Detail of library façade on rue Berri

Staircase and elevators at heart of General Collection

GRANDE BIBLIOTHÈQUE DU QUÉBEC
PATKAU ARCHITECTS WITH CROFT PELLETIER AND MENKÈS SHOONER DAGENAIS ARCHITECTES ASSOCIEÉS

Montréal, Québec, Canada
Completed 2005

An interview between Sascha Hastings (SH) and John Patkau (JP)

In 2000, Patkau Architects won an international competition to design a new central library building for the National Library of Québec. Together with a large team of architects, engineers and other specialists, principals John and Patricia Patkau designed an elegant library of green glass, copper and yellow birch that would house the library's two major collections – the General (lending) and the National (reference only). The library opened to the public in spring 2005, and since then has consistently exceeded its projected use levels, a testament to the importance of the building in Montréal, and the fact that people find it a delightful place to be. Curator Sascha Hastings talked to John Patkau from his office in Vancouver, British Columbia.

SH: Before the Grande Bibliothèque, the only other library you'd built was a small community library in suburban Surrey, BC. Why did you want to do a big library in a major urban centre like Montréal?

JP: A major library is a very interesting project. The program is rich, and there are so many different components in Montréal – the General Collection and the National Collection, plus a children's library, an auditorium, meeting rooms, an exhibition space and a very rich urban context. All of those things are wonderful material to work with as an architect and really allow you to develop a major extended piece of work, as opposed to a small project, which is often more like a short story.

Also, especially in Canada, there really are almost no public buildings anymore.

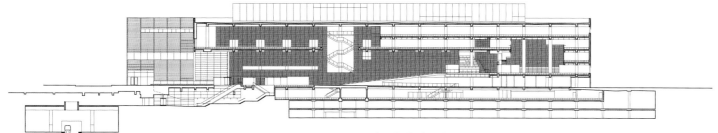

Longitudinal section through public arcade

The art gallery is public but it's focused towards a very narrow segment of the population and has a somewhat elite profile, whereas the library is the most broad-based institution and, I think, the last really democratic public building. The library has a diverse identity that addresses the community as a whole – office buildings don't do that and government buildings don't even do that. I think the average person uses a library a great deal more than they use a city hall.

SH: What did you look to for design inspiration?

JP: Even before we started the competition we had studied the whole history of library design and were well aware of precedents. My wife and I had been to libraries throughout Europe and North America, which we viewed as exemplary in some way. We'd studied libraries through architectural history, and had done a fairly exhaustive study of the building type, so we already had some very strong ideas about what would make a successful library.

SH: How did you apply these ideas to the Grande Bibliothèque?

JP: The Grande Bibliothèque is unique in that in addition to the large General Collection there's a very large National Collection, so in a sense it was like an egg with two yolks. And how you dealt with these two significant programmatic components in a way which gave them both a place and acknowledged their differences was a very interesting challenge. We had learned that libraries, in order to be accessible to the public and to facilitate the management and operation of the library, need to be fairly compact in plan, so we tried to make as cubic a library as possible in the interest of reducing distances. We also introduced the major vertical circulation system of the building in the absolute middle of the General Collection.

SH: You're talking about staircases and elevators...

JP: Right. And the purpose of that is to put you right in the middle of the collection and make your travel to the book of interest or the subject matter of interest as efficient as possible. It also facilitates the staff serving the public and maintaining the collection efficiently. But because this library has this dual nature – the double yolk – it opened the door for a secondary idea which is quite unique in the way we used it within this library, and that is that in addition to this central circulation system we developed a perimeter circulation system that begins at the entrance to the library.

SH: Is this what your wife Patricia calls the "goat path"?

JP: Yes, or the "donkey trail". So when you enter the library you have a choice – you can continue to move forward to the ground level service counters or take the stairs or elevators up to the General Collection, or you can take the stepped ramp, the "donkey trail", that goes directly to the entrance of the National Collection. And you can enter the National Collection at that point or you can turn left and continue up a terraced reading room, and then turn left again and continue along a linear reading room that overlooks rue Savoie, which is a lane that's being developed for intense

Detail of glass and copper façade

Detail of interior

pedestrian use, and then turn again and go up another terraced reading room, which takes you to the top of the library, to the last reading room. So the General Collection is effectively surrounded by reading rooms at the perimeter with natural light and views.

On the other hand, if you go into the National Collection, the opposite organizational pattern exists. You enter into a central reading room, which is surrounded by the collection, and so you have a much more formal and traditional situation where the library is organized around an interior grand reading room. In doing this we wanted to establish very strong and complementary identities for these two collections – one much more informal and casual, and the other much more static and traditional in its character, and we felt that this difference would create a very interesting juxtaposition for the major collections in the library.

SH: The Grande Bibliothèque is in the Latin Quarter – a very busy and dense part of Montréal. What are some of the ways you connect the library to the surrounding urban fabric?

JP: Libraries, by virtue of their nature, tend to be fairly insular because of the need to control access to books and who can walk away with a book, and so they typically have a single point of entrance and exit. I think that can make a very difficult urban building. So in order to offset that characteristic, we created multiple entrances and located certain aspects of the program that could exist outside the control – the auditorium, the exhibition space, the meeting rooms, the café, the library shop – outside of the library, and we made them accessible by public arcades within the building. So you can enter the library from virtually all four sides and be in this open uncontrolled public space, and so in that sense, the building is much more permeable than most libraries.

SH: There's always a difference between how architects expect people to use a building and what happens after it opens to the public. Were there any surprises for you?

JP: The library had made projections prior to the opening about use levels, and right from the beginning the use levels have been significantly higher than their projected numbers. It's intensely used – much more than they had imagined – and much to their delight, and much to our delight. I think the fact that it's such a well-used building speaks both to the importance of the institution and the need for this building in Montréal, but I think also in some measure speaks of the fact that people find the building a pleasant place to be.

Fifth level

1. General library
2. Administration
3. Staff room
4. Open to below

Fourth level

1. General library
2. Reading room
3. Collection Québécoise
4. Open to below

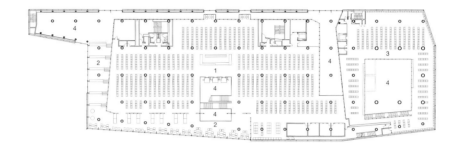

Third level

1. General library
2. Reading room
3. Map room
4. Collection Québécoise
5. Open to below

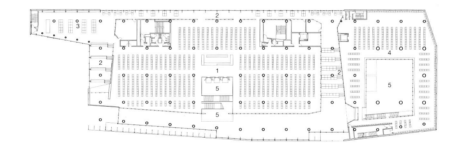

Second level

1. General library
2. Reading room
3. Collection Québécoise
4. Open to below

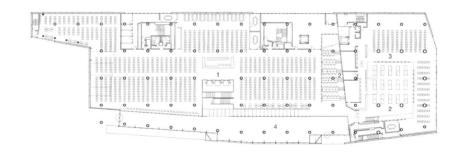

Street level

1. Main entry
2. Bookstore
3. 24/7 library
4. General library
5. Auditorium
6. Café
7. Meeting room
8. Bouquiniste
9. Open to below

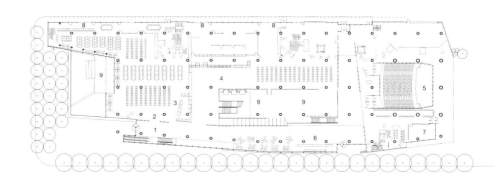

Detail of façade at night

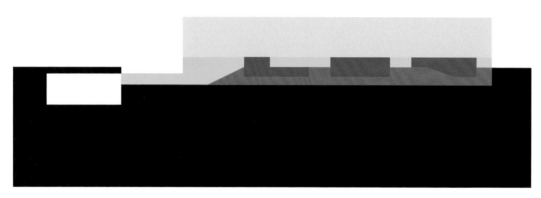

Section diagram of street and metro levels

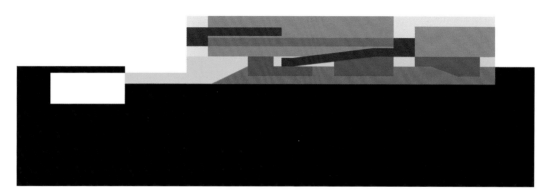

Section diagram of the two main collections linked by the promenade
that begins at the primary entrance, continues up a stepped ramp
to the entrance of the National Collection, then turns and continues alongside
the General Collection to the top of the library

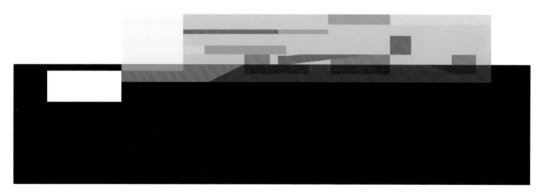

Section diagram of the glass and copper envelope that encloses
the collections, the promenade and the lower levels

DISPLACEMENTS/DÉPLACEMENTS
VOUS ÉTIEZ LÀ
DENIS FARLEY

Montréal, 2003 and 2006 respectively

Denis Farley is a Montréal artist with a background in dance. His photographic work references his interest in architecture, nature and how we inhabit these spaces, and reveals his passion for going beyond the material aspects of reality to convey elements of perception and memory.

The works in the series *Displacements/Déplacements* (2003 – 2007) touch upon the relationships between the individual and his/her presence in contemporary architectural environments. Farley integrates individuals in strategic locations and uses them as links between the volumes, spaces and materials of landmark buildings, including the modern Bibliothèque nationale de France.

In the midst of architectural details, references to nature suggest the mental space of individual projection, a kind of virtual space where thoughts can travel. Through the simple technique of image juxtaposition, the spectator is brought to question his/her cultural and emotional references. The reflective qualities of water and glass panels, for example, act as visual triggers that stimulate the passage from physical to mental states.

The quasi-symmetries of built structures unite with the human body to form a meditative choreography, which leads the viewer to question institutional values associated with architecture and to enter into a reflective state that conjures up personal memories of nature.

Vous étiez là (2006) makes use of photographs Farley took many years ago inside the Bibliothèque de Troyes in France, one of the oldest public libraries in Europe. Although these images occupied his mind and heart ever since he took them, he was unable to incorporate them into a larger piece until he saw the new Grande Bibliothèque du Québec. By combining photographs of an old library with a contemporary library, he creates an interesting effect, a sense of a shift in time and space, as though the human silhouette in the image was rethinking history.

Denis Farley, *Déplacements, Grande Bibliothèque, Paris.*
2003, digital print, edition of 5 (top)

Denis Farley, *Vous étiez là.* 2006, digital print, edition of 6 (bottom)

FROM THE ONLINE DIARY OF

DR. SAAD ESKANDER

Director of the Iraq National Library and Archive

From the website of the British Library: www.bl.uk/iraqdiary.html. Reprinted with permission.

Monday, 5 March, 2007
(This day will be always remembered, as the day when books were assassinated by the forces of darkness, hatred and fanaticism.)

The traffic was predictably very heavy. My car was searched at a checkpoint. The police officers were polite.

Miss. M. came to my office to say good byes. She has already moved to Basra, after the murder of her brother. I asked her not to be sad, as I was certain she would come back to us some time in the future.

At 9.00 someone from the Washington Post office rang me, informing me that the reporter would be a bit late. Therefore, I decided to meet the staff of the English Collections, as I planned earlier. The English Collections section is in the last floor, which [was] much more damaged than other floors. The smoke caused by the fires of mid-April 2003, dust, high temperature, the breakdown of the ventilation system and most importantly the shortage of electricity supplies took their toll on the library collections. We have around 66,300 English books in various subjects. The oldest book goes back to 1845. Twelve librarians work in the English collection section, and all of them speak English. The inventorying work has started in September 2005 when three librarians undertook to make new cataloguing cards [to] replace the missing ones [lost] during the mid-April fires in 2003. They had also to classify, catalogue, correct past mistakes and clean hundreds of other books. It has been a very difficult task, as the books storage area had no air conditioning system for several months. The old conditioning system had been removed during the Saddam Rule for unknown reasons! The frequent power cuts, especially in the summer, make it very difficult to work inside the books storage area. However, my staff went on doing their task, even when the temperature rose to 48 centigrade. During the meeting, they complained about the power cuts, temperature and the dust. They asked me to provide them with good gloves, pens and white inks. Towards the end of the meeting, the head of the security of the building informed me that two people (one foreigner and one Iraqi) were waiting for me. I told him to take both men immediately to my office, and that I would meet them in 5 minutes.

I introduced myself to the Washington Post reporter and his Iraqi colleague, before the interview. I was asked various questions about culture in general and INLA in particular. We talked frankly about the security situation and impact on the INLA and its staff, etc.

As we were talking, a huge explosion shook the INLA's building around 11.35. We, the three of us, ran to the nearest window, and we saw a big and thick grey smoke rising from the direction of al-Mutanabi Street, which is less than 500 meters away from the INLA. I learnt later that the explosion was a result of a car bomb attack. Tens of thousands of papers were flying high, as if the sky was raining books, tears and blood. The view was surreal. Some of the papers were burning in the sky. Many burning pieces of papers fell on the INLA's building. Al-Mutanabi Street is named after one of the greatest Arab poets, who lived in Iraq in the middle ages. The Street is one of [the] well-known areas of Baghdad and where many publishing houses, printing companies and bookstores have their main offices and storages. Its old cafés are the most favorite place for the impoverished intellectuals, who get their inspirations and ideas from this very old quarter of Baghdad. The street is also famous for its Friday's book market, where secondhand, new and rare books are sold and purchased. The INLA purchases about 95% of new publications from al-Mutanabi Street. I also buy my own books from the same street. It was extremely sad to learn that a number of the publishers and book sellers, whom we knew very well, were among the dead, including Mr. Adnan, who was supposed to deliver a consignment of new publications to the INLA. According to an early estimation, more than 30 people were killed and 100 more injured. Four brothers were killed in their office.

Immediately after the explosion, I ordered the guards to prevent all my staff from leaving the building, as there was a possibility of another bomb attack. My staff and I were watching the movement of a number [of] civilian and military ambulances, carrying killed and injured people. It was a heartbreaking view.

Almost ten minutes after the explosion, the Washington Post's reporter and his Iraqi colleague left the building. Their destination was unsurprisingly al-Mutanabi Street, the site of the massacre. Before the end of the meeting, we agreed to meet again next morning to continue the interview. After I arrived to my home, my wife told me that a big bomb blast shook our house at 11.30 and that dust and smoke covered our neighborhood. Fortunately, no one was hurt.

At 18.10, I was the guest of a Spanish radio [station] that broadcasts to Spain and Latin America. I answered by phone [a] series of questions about the INLA, its staff and the security challenges. The interview lasted 15 minutes.

Almost one hour later, the Reuters reporter in Baghdad rang me, asking me some question about the al-Mutanabi Street's car bomb attack, its history and cultural importance.

I watched the night news bulletin. The car bomb attack against Al-Mutanabia shocked all Iraqis regardless of their religious and ethnic background. The President, the Prime Minster and some other high-rank officials condemned the attack. Our political leaders are the best when it comes to the 'extremely difficult' task of issuing condemnation statements, while the annihilation of our culture and intellectual class goes on before their very eyes everyday.

At 20.25, my brother rang from London, asking me if everybody was fine. I reassured him that we all were fine. Then, as usual, we talked about politics, our friends and families.

PUBLIC

"There is not such a cradle of democracy upon the earth as the Free Public Library."

ANDREW CARNEGIE

THE PUBLIC LIBRARY

Many people acquire their first impressions of a library from their local public library. At one time, that might have meant a rather dark and dusty building presided over by stern-faced women in tweed who didn't hesitate to shush you if you spoke above a whisper. The public library has come a long way since then. Many boast bright, open spaces, or are housed in modern architectural structures. The array of programs available at the public library has also changed dramatically. In addition to their traditional mandate of loaning books, films and music recordings, many public libraries function as cultural or civic centres, hosting classes, workshops and community events, and offering access to the Internet. The public library is also universal in its acceptance of visitors from every social strata and ethnic or religious group.

The most significant public library movement in history was started by Scottish-American industrialist and philanthropist Andrew Carnegie. Born in Dunfermline, Scotland in 1835, Carnegie and his family moved to Allegheny, Pennsylvania in 1848. Over the next decades, Carnegie made a fortune in railways, iron, oil and especially steel. However, Carnegie believed that the wealthy should give back to society, and in 1881 began propagating his idea of free public libraries when he donated the funds for a library in Dunfermline. Over the next 36 years, Carnegie spent more than $56 million to build 2,509 libraries throughout the English-speaking world, including 125 in Canada (111 located in Ontario).[1] Carnegie's faith in the power of public libraries was due in large part to his own experience as a young man in Allegheny, where a Colonel James Anderson had opened his private library to local "working boys" on Saturdays. The young Andrew Carnegie passed many hours there, and credited much of his future success to those days he spent educating himself in the colonel's library.

In order to be granted a Carnegie Library, a town was required to apply for the funds, which were usually approved, provided that the town demonstrated a need for a library, agreed to donate the building site and committed to covering ongoing operational expenses. The architecture of Carnegie Libraries varied in style and complexity, but they all shared a prominent main entrance, usually accessed by steps (to give the visitor the sense of elevating himself), a central reference desk, a reading room and open stacks. Carnegie thus believed that he was offering every young man the opportunity to make a success of himself – if he was industrious and ambitious enough to make use of the library.

In Canada, the first Carnegie Library was built in Windsor, Ontario in 1903. Although it and several other Canadian Carnegie Libraries have since been demolished, many are still in use as libraries, while others have been converted to meet changing community needs.

In this section we will look at two Canadian Carnegie Libraries – the Hespeler Library in Cambridge, Ontario, which was recently renovated by Kongats Architects Inc., and the former Barrie Public Library, which has been converted into a modern art gallery – the MacLaren Art Centre – by Hariri Pontarini Architects. In addition, artist Guy Laramée contributes a story and an art work about a community of people known as the "Biblios", but we begin with an essay by acclaimed American writer Ray Bradbury, who attributes his successful career and personal happiness to free public libraries.

The Windsor Public Library, ca. 1905

---

1. http://www.culture.gov.on.ca/english/culdiv/library/carnegie.htm

Andrew Carnegie in his study

LIBRARIES, THE LOVE OF MY LIFE
RAY BRADBURY

In my last year at L.A. High School I was not much of a creative student; I didn't know how to write a decent poem, my short stories were nothing at all and my essays were almost non-existent, but somehow I had a kind of dream about myself and my future.

When my picture appeared in the annual in my graduation month they asked me to give them three quotes about myself. The first quote was: Admired as a thespian. The second quote: Likes to write stories. The third quote: Headed for literary distinction.

Now how could I have said that? It's simply incredible, isn't it, since I was nowhere at all at the moment and my relationship with teachers in High School had been with just two teachers, Jennet Johnson, who taught me the short story, and Snow Longley Housh who loved poetry.

Beyond that I discovered the way I wanted to learn was face-to-face meetings with teachers and not sitting in a classroom.

I put all of my credits in at L.A. City College, hoping to take lessons there in becoming a writer and during the summer after high school I took a night course in writing short stories.

After three weeks of that it was so incredibly boring that I dropped out because I wanted to work alone, for me.

Then, facing up to L.A. City College, what were my further thoughts? The reason I was going to college was, let's face it, young women. Now that's not a proper reason to go to school.

I wanted to become a writer and I finally settled on a really good solution, which would allow me to become a creative person. The answer, of course, was libraries.

So I had a one-to-one relationship with libraries all over Los Angeles; the local one, a few blocks from the house, and the major one, in downtown L.A., a big cement structure, which was exciting to just run through.

Do you hear how I put that? I simply didn't walk through, but ran from room to room, seeking a home, seeking the silence in which I could have the proper thoughts.

My two favorite rooms became the fiction room, which contained hundreds of novels covering a period of fifty to sixty years, and the literary room, across from it, which was full of the lives of authors, their biographies, autobiographies, the right books of criticism and volumes of plays and poetry; I began to move from one room to the other and my visits to libraries occurred two to three times a week.

Every morning I would run to my typewriter to be alone with me. I realized that I would never sit in a classroom again because I didn't want to be surrounded by students who were nothing like me, nor was there a chance for a personal relationship with the teacher upfront.

I needed friendship. Either an architectural friendship, which was the library or along the way, perhaps some other person wandering into one of those rooms and colliding with me.

During the next ten years I spent almost every day in the library, brooding on the silence, enjoying the vibration that came out of the walls that were chock full of books and filled with the library life of authors who had been in love with living and creation.

The library became my favorite place to read. It was good to read at home or in a park, but the library was a special, embryonic place where a person could sit with the vibration of lives off the walls, all around him.

During that ten year period I wrote a short story every single week and hundreds of short stories collected, of varying quality. Those at the beginning were not much at all, but along the way I picked up the lives and the vibrations of the great authors and began slowly to believe in myself.

By the time I was twenty-three I began to publish my first short stories in science fiction magazines and *Weird Tales* and was paid the incredibly high amount of fifteen dollars a story!

But I was still a long way off from the heights where existed *Harpers Magazine, The Atlantic Monthly,* and all the wonderful intellectual literary gazettes, where I wished to exist.

I had a young friend with personal problems who went to a psychiatrist looking for cures. I became curious about him and his relationship and I said, "You know, it seems to me I need to talk to your psychiatrist just one time. I don't believe people should have relationships with psychiatrists that go on for months or years, which proves it's not working if it has to go on that long. I want one meeting. Can you arrange that?"

He said, "It costs thirty dollars for fifty minutes. When do you want to do this?"

"Tomorrow," I said.

He arranged the time and, dragging my feet I walked from the library to the psychiatrist's office and sat across from him.

He said, "How can I help you? Can you state your problem?"

I thought for a moment and it suddenly burst from my lips: "I hope you can help me. I want to be the greatest writer that ever lived." There must have been an exclamation point at the end of that declaration.

The psychiatrist looked stunned and I thought I heard him laugh quietly for a moment and there was a strange smile on his face – I can imagine how he must have talked of me and my declaration when he went home that night to his wife. I listened to the echo of myself and tried to remember exactly what I had said: I want to be the greatest writer that ever lived. What an egotistical declaration!

The psychiatrist paused for a moment and then said, "Let me suggest to you that you look at the lives of all the greatest writers that ever were. Go to the library and go to the *Encyclopedia Brittanica* and read their lives and discover how soon they became known or how soon they became permanently unknown. Maybe you can learn from that. I wish you well."

I walked away from my first and last meeting with the psychiatrist, blushing from what I had said. But on the other hand I went to the library and opened the encyclopedia and looked up the lives of Tolstoy and Dickens and Shakespeare to see how they had forged through the world and to wonder how I could, in some way, emulate them.

Well, what I had just said to the psychiatrist caused me to hasten even more to the library, because I had made such a fool of myself and remembered what I had put in the *L.A. High Annual,* declaring my future as a writer.

I more and more went and stayed at the library and assimilated and began to meet other writers in one-to-one relationships so that I could learn how they were behaving.

Most importantly, however, was when I was still in high school I found Somerset Maugham's wonderful book, *The Summing Up.* In a very calm and quiet voice he told me of the path up ahead, not to be influenced from left to right, so that my career varied, but to go straight ahead to find myself.

The second book that I discovered was *Becoming A Writer,* by Dorothea Brande, whose marvelous essays opened up my psyche.

So you can see, I found a good part of myself among all the books.

In the years from 1941 to 1946 I went every Sunday at noon to Muscle Beach in Santa Monica, where my dear friend and teacher, Leigh Brackett, went to be with the body builders and to rest up from her weekly writing for *Planet Stories* and, finally, doing a screenplay for Howard Hawkes at Warner Brothers.

After three hundred meetings with Leigh Brackett at the beach, talking face-to-face about possible literature and life, I began to move up slowly into the future of literature.

I had tried to forget how dumb I had been with the psychiatrist and simply went back to the library and walled myself in with books and got to know the two women in charge of those two special rooms, knowing that if I ever published a book the first people I would give a copy of my book to would be those two librarians.

Finally I began to write stories of such quality that began to appear in the bigger magazines and I became assured of a somewhat uneasy future with my talent.

My education in the library then was complete. I knew that I couldn't learn how to write in a high school or a college or a night school. I knew that I had to be my own teacher and pick up the fragments of information from the walls of the downtown library and from the library a few blocks away from my house.

So the library was the center of my life. I didn't go there for the young women who beckoned me, but I had hopes along the way, perhaps, to meet just one woman who had the qualities of a librarian, an English teacher, or a seller of books.

I found just such a wonderful young woman at Fowler Brothers bookstore in downtown L.A. where she sold me a book, looked in my face and read my first short story in an anthology.

When I came back to see her, she redirected me to the library and to all the books on the shelves of the store where she lived her creative selling life.

So it was complete: my movement through the world, writing, and going to the library, and finding a young woman who was a book person.

After a long engagement, because we were both relatively poor, we finally married and settled in Venice, California, where I went to the library there and finally published my first book of short stories and my first novel.

I ended up writing my most important novel where? I went to the library at UCLA and found a typing room in the basement of the library where I could rent a typewriter for ten cents a half-hour.

Surrounded by students with whom I had no contact, I sat alone and isolated at my typewriter and spent $9.80 in dimes and wrote *Fahrenheit 451* over a period of nine days.

In the library! What a place to write my most important book. I ran up and down stairs in a passion, in a white-hot temper, and did the book in full dash and published it out of mad love for literature.

I had finally made that first big step toward the future. Was I becoming the greatest writer that ever lived? Hardly that. I had long since forgotten what I had declared for myself, but I was locked in the library where my most important book had been born.

So there you have it. Not schools of any sort, not teachers of any sort, except other writers who lived a life of love for writing, and writing every day and going back to the library when my first book was published to deliver copies to those two librarians in the fiction and literary section because simply by handing me books and telling me what to read, they had become my prime teachers.

There it is: The love of my life, libraries, which created me and gave me birth.

For them I give back my love.

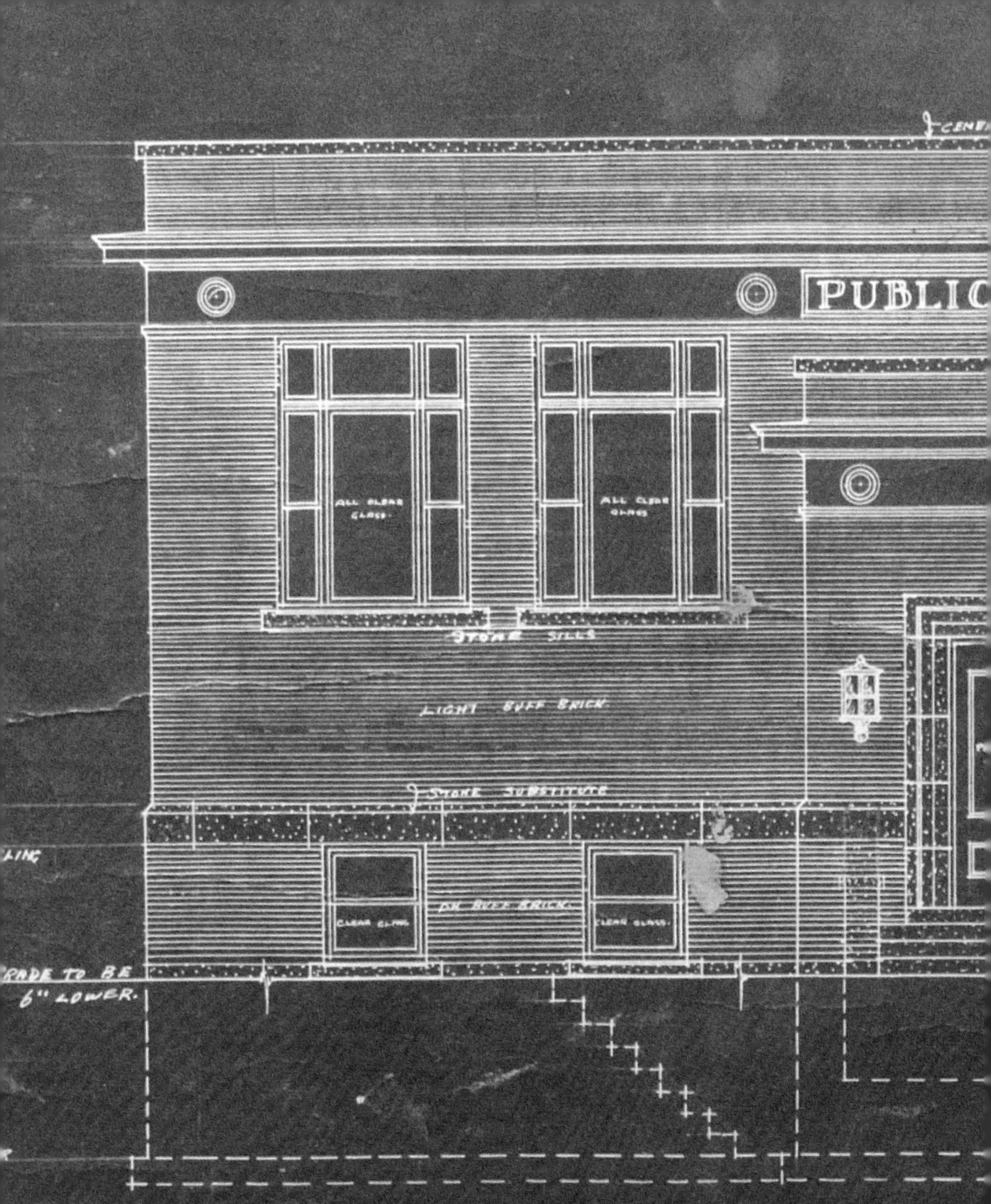

PUBLIC

ALL CLEAR
GLASS

ALL CLEAR
GLASS

STONE SILLS

LIGHT BUFF BRICK

STONE SUBSTITUTE

DK BUFF BRICK

CLEAR GLASS

CLEAR GLASS

LING

GRADE TO BE
6" LOWER.

Original front elevation blueprint of 1922 Carnegie Public Library, Hespeler, Ontario

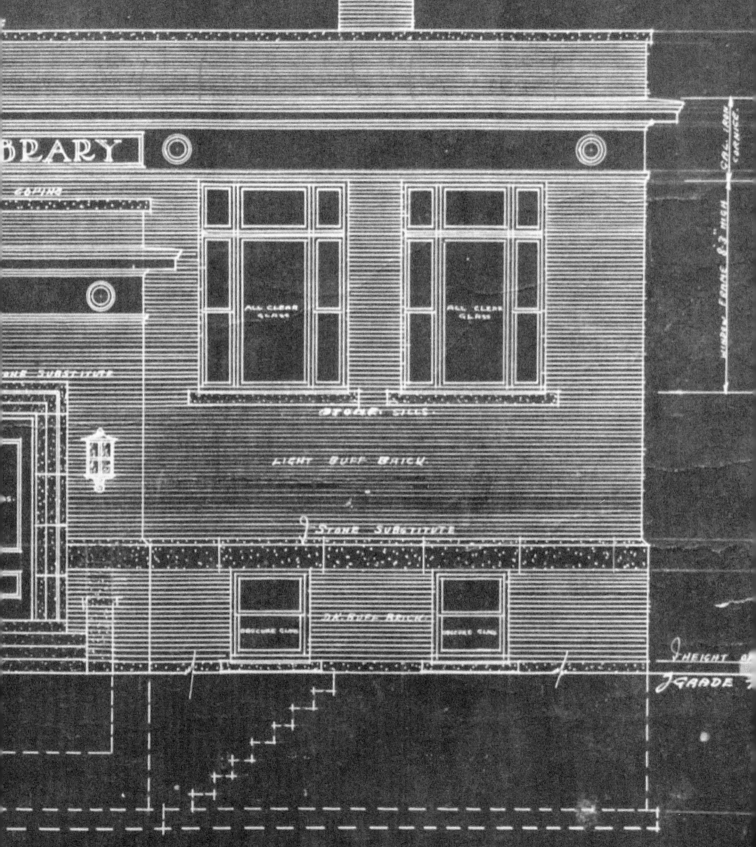

The new Hespeler "library inside a library" viewed in its entirety

HESPELER LIBRARY
KONGATS ARCHITECTS INC.

Cambridge, Ontario, Canada
Completed 2007

An interview between Sascha Hastings (SH) and Alar Kongats (AK)

The Hespeler Library in the town of Hespeler (amalgamated into the City of Cambridge in 1973), Ontario was founded as a Mechanics' Institute in 1871. The collection was housed in various locations until it found a permanent home in a building constructed in 1922 with a grant of $14,500 from the Carnegie Foundation. In spite of major renovations to the library in 1984 and again in 1992, the library could not keep up with growing demand, so Cambridge Libraries and Galleries invited several firms to submit proposals for an extensive renovation. Kongats Architects Inc. won the competition with its daring design for a "library inside a library", which enclosed the original Carnegie Library in a glass box. The Hespeler Library re-opened in June 2007. Shortly thereafter, curator Sascha Hastings talked to principal architect Alar Kongats in his Toronto office.

SH: The most notable feature of the Hespeler Library is a glass skin that encapsulates the old Carnegie Library. What inspired this?

AK: Cambridge has a longstanding historical association with textile manufacturing and design. During World War II, Dominion Textiles was the biggest textile mill in the British Empire and today Cambridge Libraries and Galleries have a mandate to collect, nurture and promote contemporary textile art, so the skin of the building pays homage to all that. Although the skin is glass, it's multi-layered, with two patterns that run around the outside – one is a set of fritted ceramic rectangles tattooed onto the glass and the other, a repeating series of fine vertical lines. These patterns do different things – the rectangular pattern gives the glass a sense of materiality, like a surface weaving or printing.

It also means the outside skin isn't a neutral skin, but one in which varying densities of frit highlight views to the outside or intensify a sense of enclosure to interior spaces. The other pattern is like a woven piece of yarn, which is consistent throughout the skin and helps neutralize the transition from something that is more transparent to something that is more opaque and solid. There's also a third layer – the draperies by Armstrong Fox Textiles. They are so tactile, and they filter the light that comes into the building, so I see them as very much a part of the exterior skin of the building.

We wanted something that was taut, almost like athletic wear – trim, layered, able to ventilate, with very few extraneous details – that stretches around the building like a wrapper. In our climate we tend to wear our clothing in layers, so it also seemed natural to layer the skin and allow for natural ventilation, which is something you don't typically get in libraries anymore.

SH: Can you tell me about the other features of the library?

AK: Community libraries generally have common requirements – they have a program or community-use room, a children's area, a computer area, a stack area, a reading room, a magazine area and a reference room, so we obviously needed to accommodate all these functions. Typically these functions in new libraries today tend to be one-floor plans, unencumbered in their openness and spatially neutral, somewhat warehouse-like. The intent, I gather, in addition to visibility, is one of flexibility to allow one program function to migrate into an adjacent program area

depending on shifts in functional demands. But this means something always gets sacrificed for something else, which to me isn't real flexibility.

We had the luxury of the existing Carnegie Library providing a major room on both floors, each with its own defined qualities of volume, light, scale, containment and view. The stacks are contained within the upper level of the Carnegie so they couldn't just creep into, say, the reading room and diminish the original setting of that room. Not having space you can just shift around all the time adds to a sense of stability, which I think is one of the reasons people go to libraries – it isn't just a warehouse that becomes a virtual reality space in which you become totally disassociated from the outside world.

In the Hespeler Library you have a view to the outside or to the fireplace in the reading room, or in the kids' area they're surrounded by the old Carnegie foundation walls, so that each area has its own specific architectural characteristics and qualities of space that typically don't exist in new libraries. The grand reading room also reinforces the idea of community, which is probably another reason people go to libraries, even though so much information is now available online.

SH: What appealed to you most about building a public library?

AK: I think community libraries are one of the last bastions of free public buildings. You don't have to pay a user fee, you can go almost any time of the day, you can feel reasonably comfortable and know you're not going to get kicked out, and you

Interior detail with new glass skin at left and original 1922 building at right (top)
The library at dusk (bottom)

Second floor reading room with draperies by Armstrong Fox Textiles

Second floor reading area with fireplace

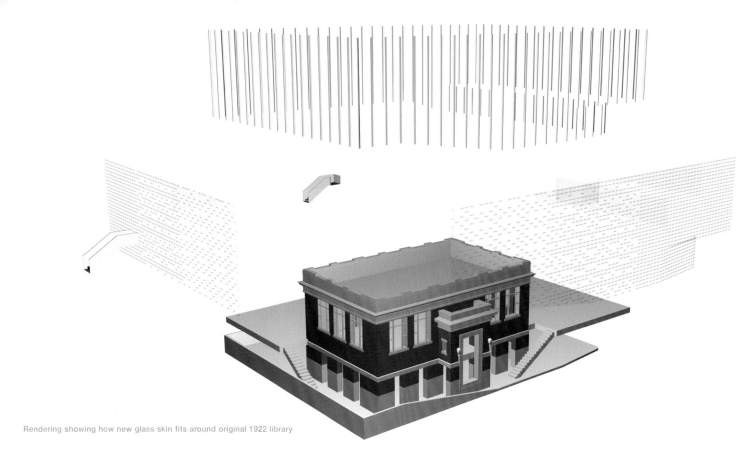

Rendering showing how new glass skin fits around original 1922 library

can search out the information or pleasure you want and there's nobody to tell you not to. The fact is, the library is a pretty censorship-free area. And no one tells you what you can wear. For example, last week when we were shooting some photographs at Hespeler a mother came in with her two young children and they were dressed in their pajamas. And we asked what was going on and she said "Oh, they're just coming to pick up their night-time reading". So there's this sense that the library, having this domesticated comfort zone, is not a whole lot different in terms of how you can use it than your own home. I'm not sure that exists in any other public institution.

SH: What kind of impact do you think the Hespeler Library will have on the larger community?
AK: The City of Cambridge is looking at how to revitalize downtown Hespeler and make it a more interesting place, and they very wisely want to make use of its natural attributes, which are the river that runs through the town and some of the old industrial buildings. So the library reinforces the importance of the downtown area and sends the signal to private enterprise that the city's going to invest in it. The library also has an immediate benefit because of its heavy public use, meaning it helps sustain the coffee shop or the wrap shop up on Queen Street. So I think to build something that is iconic for Hespeler and that people might see as an attraction was

very important. This sort of thing isn't atypical for small European towns, but in Canada we often diminish our own rich architectural heritage. For a number of years my family lived in Dundas, which has a very rich architecture, so I know there are a lot of wonderful things within these communities! But instead, we go to Europe, and we visit charming little towns there, but in fact they're not much different from Hespeler. We just don't realize it has value as a built environment or see it as something that other people might want to come to, and so we don't market it as that. So I think that the Hespeler Library is reinforcing the idea that it's worth doing something well because it can have a bigger impact in terms of the wider community.

SH: Do you have a favourite space in the library?
AK: I have lots, but the reading room is where I could easily spend an afternoon – it reminds me of the Four Seasons Restaurant in New York. It is modern yet classical in its proportions – the columns encapsulating the space, the curtains, the wood floors, the luxe red chairs – they all in a way speak to an older, more gracious and old-fashioned time, like when the original Carnegie Library was built back in 1922. It's kind of nice, because it allows those people who maybe can't get to the Four Seasons to enjoy an equally nice space in Hespeler.

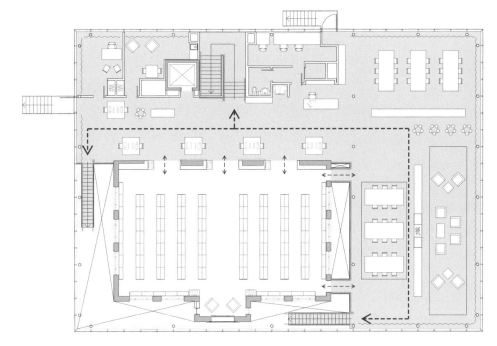

Second floor plan

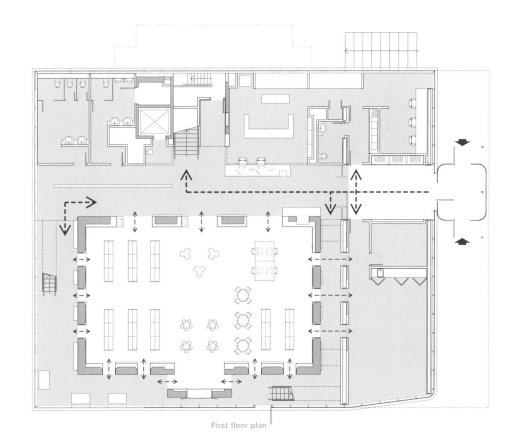

First floor plan

The Hespeler Library at night (left) with old town hall (right)

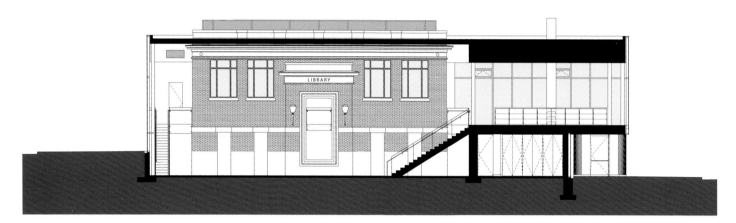

Section through new glass volume, with elevation of historic library within

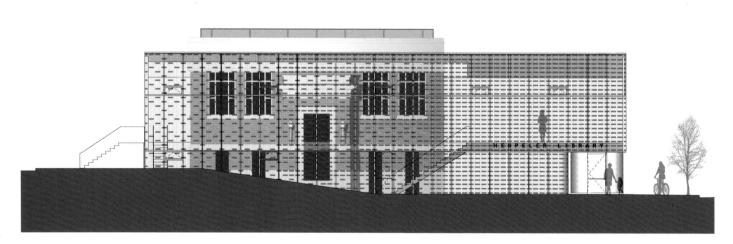

Elevation showing new glass enclosure

Main entry with weather canopy

MACLAREN ART CENTRE
HARIRI PONTARINI ARCHITECTS

Barrie, Ontario, Canada
Completed 2001

The MacLaren Art Centre is a superb example of a sensitive contemporary architectural intervention on a former Carnegie Library, converting it to a new use. The original building was completed in 1917 with funds from the Carnegie Corporation of New York. Its Palladian style doors and windows, acanthus leaf bracketed keystones, and combination of red brick, terra-cotta and Indiana limestone make it quite typical of classical revival style Carnegie Libraries in Ontario.

In 1964, architects Pentland and Baker and Salter and Allison designed a new wing, which included brick patterns and large arched windows similar to those in the original building.

The building continued to function as the Barrie Public Library until the late 1990s, when the library moved into a new, much larger building. The City of Barrie hired Toronto-based Hariri Pontarini Architects to renovate the former Carnegie building as the new home for the MacLaren Art Centre, comprised of a public art gallery, retail shop, café and several multi-purpose rooms.

The renovations were completed in the summer of 2001, and the building re-opened in late September. This library-turned-art gallery is a beautiful open blend of old and new.

Main entry

Public space, second floor, showing juxtaposition between old and new

View into gift shop

Carnegie Gallery

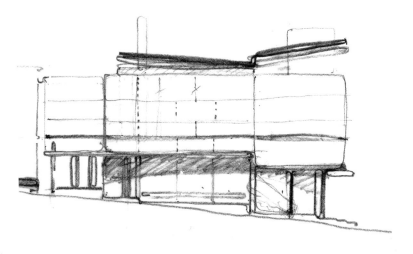

Construction image, with the original building at left, and formwork at right

The new steel frame under construction, with the original building in the background

BIBLIOS

GUY LARAMÉE

Montréal, 2001 (sculpture) and 2004 (story)
Excerpted and edited from a longer story by Guy Laramée

Once upon a time, a long time ago, there were people who collected words. They were called the Biblios. They had all sorts of words, and plenty of them.

When words were lacking, they invented new ones. Words were not only to name things, they were also used to create new things. For example, one day someone would wake up and proclaim: Software! and there it was.

The Biblios were so fond of words that they began connecting them together. For example by connecting "Cyclops" and "Pedestrian", they had invented the word "Encyclopedia", which originally meant "to walk with one eye shut".

The Biblios connected words by digging tunnels between words. By digging their way to new words, every day the Biblios were adding to a vast network of tunnels. The Biblios were divided in two groups. There were those who dug horizontally and those who dug vertically. The Horizontals covered much terrain but their words lacked depth. The Verticals found very few words, but these words were more penetrating. One group of marginals tried to dig diagonally, but they were outcast. The Biblios were constantly forced to dig new tunnels. What started as a passion had now become a necessity.

In the beginning, the Biblios were nomads. They liked to travel to find new words and to hear the collections of their neighbours. Words were very useful things. You could bring them anywhere. The Biblios put their words on little chains. First they wore the chains around their necks like collars, but after a while they became too heavy to carry.

The Biblios started to line up their collections in big notebooks, a bit like what stamp collectors do. Each day at sunset they would come to contemplate their collection, and they would add the words that their hunting had brought them. For the Biblios were great word hunters. As their collections grew, the Biblios put their words into bigger and bigger notepads, then into albums, and then into books.

Their collection grew even bigger, and now they needed a catalogue. A catalogue is a collection of collections. The Biblios were now realizing that the characteristic feature of collections is that they are never complete! That's what makes collections exciting. That's also what makes them a major cause of anxiety. By dint, the Biblios ended up constituting enormous libraries and there was no place left for anything else.

The problem was that the tunnels were undermining the foundation of the libraries. The Biblios realized that words were disappearing, but not solely because of the digging. Distressingly, words were aging. Words were like biological organisms: they would be born, they would grow and they would die…

The Biblios had started to fear for their collections. What would happen if a collection was to disappear? The majority of them had settled the problem by believing that the collections that were disappearing went into another library, a larger one, somewhere in the earth, maybe in the centre of the world. Others started to look for other, less fragile mediums to store their words. They began to engrave words in aluminium grooves (to protect the collections from savage digging), and then put them in glass mummies (called Coffins of Disclosures, or CDs). Despite this, words were still dying and so was the whole of the Biblios civilization.

As their world was slipping through their fingers, the Biblios tried one last time to save their files. They looked desperately for the magic antidote that would keep their words from destroying one another.

But it was too late. There were already too many holes in their story.

In the end, scholars generally agree that the Biblios civilization collapsed under the weight of its knowledge.[1]

---

1. However, there is a small group of academics who believe that the Biblios never existed
    and that one can invent all kinds of stories with words.

Guy Laramée, *Biblios*. 2001, eroded books, basswood, MDF

PRIVATE

"Come, and take choice of all my library, and so beguile thy sorrow…"

SHAKESPEARE ~ *Titus Andronicus*

083

THE PRIVATE LIBRARY

A private library inevitably reflects the personality of its owner – likes and dislikes, strengths and weaknesses, and self-image. Often it is an accidental self-portrait that is painted over many years. In some cases, the connective threads – the circumstances of acquisition, or the emotional attachments and memories vested in specific books – are made available to an outside observer through personal writings or bills of sale. In others, the secrets may never be revealed to anyone but the collector.

Some private libraries are created as a respite or shield against the chaos of the world. Others appear to have been compiled with deliberate purpose, perhaps with the ambition of constructing a predetermined identity, or a wish to be seen as an expert in a certain field of study. These libraries may also reflect an affinity for a particular time or place.

As writer Philipp Blom states, books "have a voice with which they speak across time and across lives.... They are at once relics of a different era and personalities forever in the prime of their life, talking as objects and as books, from their own time and from that of the reader's."[1]

Collectors of old and rare books sometimes see themselves as crusaders, "saving" unloved or under-appreciated books. Some collectors even cross over into bibliomania, and will go to great lengths, great expense and sometimes great risk to add a book to their collection, and then another, and another. Yet others treat private libraries as a sales tool – advertisers, realtors and even interior designers have used book-lined shelves to sell everything from beer to expensive condominiums, knowing full well that there are plenty of consumers who wish to benefit from the instant aura of class that a private library confers.

Regardless of the nature of your own library, sharing it with another person is an intensely intimate experience. It's like baring your soul, and carries the risk, as in any intimate encounter, of being judged and found lacking in some way. Again, to quote Philipp Blom, "Show me your library and I'll tell you who you are."[2]

Logotopia provides the opportunity to glimpse into several types of private libraries. Discover a novella by Uruguayan writer Carlos Maria Dominguez, interpretive artworks by artists Douglas Coupland and Michael Lewis, and two recent bricks and mortar examples designed by Shigeru Ban Architects and Shim-Shutcliffe Architects. This section begins with an essay by writer Alberto Manguel, who has devoted his life to books and reading, and who invites us into his private library.

Vintage magazine ad for Schlitz Beer

1. Philipp Blom, *To Have and To Hold: An Intimate History of Collectors and Collecting* (Woodstock, New York: The Overlook Press, 2003), 200.

2. Ibid., 201.

EX LIBRIS

BEDŘICH BENEŠ

Ex libris of Bedřich Beneš, by Max Schenke. Engraving, date unknown

SKOPEČKOVA KNIHOVNA

GLADYS·B·SKOPECEK

MY LIBRARY
ALBERTO MANGUEL

Ex libris of Eugen Eichmann, by Frans Masereel
Woodcut, date unknown

A library is an ideally-suited place for our gloomy times. Wandering through the stacks of one of the world's great libraries, the Biblioteca Nacional of Buenos Aires, Jorge Luis Borges once imagined that the millions of volumes around him constituted not a model of the universe but the universe itself, its doppelgänger as it were. The idea is thrilling: that everything we know, that everything we believe we can know of this chaotic world, might be reflected in an orderly way on the open shelves of a library. I can think of no other place that justifies such jubilant optimism.

If every library is a model of the universe, then mine is a reduced version of that model, a lesser individual of the colossal species. During the day, its resemblance to the real thing is deceiving. Down and across the lettered passages, I move with a visible purpose in search of a name or a voice, calling books to my attention according to their allotted rank and file. The structure of the place is visible: a maze not to become lost in but to find, a divided room that follows an apparently logical sequence of classification, obedient to a predetermined table of contents and a memorable hierarchy of alphabets and numbers. But at night, the atmosphere changes. Sounds become muffled, thoughts grow louder. Time seems closer to that moment halfway between wakefulness and sleep in which the world can be deliberately reimagined. My movements feel unwittingly furtive, my activity secret. I turn into something of a ghost. The books are now the real presence and it is I, their reader, who, through cabalistic rituals of half-glimpsed letters, is conjured up and lured to a certain volume and a certain page. The order decreed by the catalogues is, at night, merely conventional, it holds no prestige in the shadows. Free from quotidian constraints, unobserved, my eyes and hands roam across the tidy rows restoring chaos. One book calls to another unexpectedly, creating alliances across different cultures and centuries. A half-remembered line is echoed by another of which sober concordances tell me, in the light of day, nothing. If the library in the morning suggests a mirror of the severe and reasonable order of the world, the library at night seems to rejoice in the world's essential, joyful muddle.

The library at night is not for every reader. Michel de Montaigne, for instance, disagreed with my preference. His library (he spoke of *librairie,* not *bibliothèque,* since the use of these words was just beginning to change in the vertiginous 16th century) stood on the third floor of his tower, lodged in a disaffected closet. "I spend there most of the days of my life and most of the hours of the day: I am never there at night." At night, Montaigne slept, since he believed that the body suffered enough for the sake of the reading mind. "Books have many pleasant qualities for those who know how to choose them; but there is no good without effort: it is not a plain and pure pleasure, not more so than others; it has its disagreements, and they are onerous; the soul disports itself, but the body, whose care I have not forgotten, remains inactive, it grows weary and sad."

The library in which I have at long last collected my books began life as a barn, here in la Vienne, sometime in the 15th century. When I first saw it, forming one of the branches of a U-shaped string of buildings, all that was left was a single stone wall, separating the property from a chicken run and the neighbour's field. According to village legend, before it held the barn, the wall belonged to one of the two castles that Tristan l'Hermite, minister of Louis XI of France and notorious for his cruelty, built for his sons around 1433. The first of the castles still stands, much altered during the 18th century. The second burned down and the only wall left standing, with a pigeon tower attached to its far end, became the property of the Church,

Interior of Alberto Manguel's library

cutting off one side of the presbytery garden. In 1693, the inhabitants of the village ("gathered outside the church doors" says the deed) granted the incumbent priest permission to wall in the old cemetery and plant a small orchard over the emptied tombs. At the same time, the castle wall was used to erect a new barn. After the French Revolution, storms, war and neglect caused the barn to crumble, and even after services resumed in the church in 1837, and a new priest came to live in the presbytery, the barn was not rebuilt. The ancient wall continued to serve merely as a property divider, looking onto a farmer's field on one side and shading a magnolia tree and bushes of hydrangea on the other.

As soon as I saw the wall, I knew that here was where I would build the room to house my books. I wanted a room panelled in dark wood, with soft pools of light and comfortable chairs. Ideally, I imagined shelves that began at my waist and went only as high as the fingertips of my stretched-out arm, since the books relinquished to heights that require ladders or to depths that force the reader to crawl on the floor receive far less attention than their middle-ground fellows. But these ideal arrangements would have required a library three or four times the size of the vanished barn and, as Robert Louis Stevenson so mournfully put it, "that is the bitterness of art: you see a good effect, and some nonsense about sense continually intervenes." So my library has shelves that begin just above the running-boards and that end an octavo away from the beams of the slanted ceiling. At night, if the moon is out, the intimate lighting of the place is perfect. Paradise sometimes must adapt itself to suit circumstantial requirements.

Setting up a library after many years of change is akin to writing an autobiography. The order, the atmosphere, the titles that have survived moves, thefts, acts of God, oblivion in the hands of absent-minded friends, trace the pattern of something that resembles our life. My geography is in these pages: Buenos Aires, Paris, London, the vastness of Canada, the always far-away South Seas. I am grateful that chance has allowed me to set up my books in this secret corner of France where I hope, one day, my ghost, in the dark, may still turn the yellowing pages.

Ex libris of Helmut Arndt, by Helmut Arndt
Woodcut, date unknown

Interior of Alberto Manguel's library

LIBRARY OF A POET
SHIGERU BAN ARCHITECTS

Kanagawa, Japan
Completed 1991

Library with loft in centre

Shigeru Ban is an architect born in Tokyo in 1957. His firm, Shigeru Ban Architects, is based in Tokyo, with offices in New York and Paris. He is particularly known for his innovative use of organic materials such as paper, bamboo and engineered wood. Although Ban had built temporary structures of paper tubes in Nagoya (1989) and Odawara (1990), Library of a Poet was Ban's first permanent building made of paper tubes.

Shigeru Ban was not available for a telephone interview. However, he sent the following statement about Library of a Poet:

"This library was built as an annex to the House for a Poet, which had been previously extended and improved by the architect. The project's genesis was based on the insight of the owner, who having seen the Odawara Pavilion, expressed his opinion that 'since books were made from paper, it would be a good idea to make a paper library'. It was decided to employ a development of the paper-tube truss used in the East Gate at Odawara. In this case the tubes were 10 cm in diameter and 12.5 mm thick, slightly smaller than those used at Odawara, but in a similar way post-tensioned steel wires were used for the spanning sections. Previously we had used steel angles to form the joints whereas here we employed 10 cm square timber pieces. The four full-height bookshelves that are ranged along the sides are structurally independent of the paper tubes and are cantilevered from the floor, absorbing the horizontal loads. The bookshelves, which contain insulating material and have an exterior finish, were fabricated separately in the factory."

South façade at night

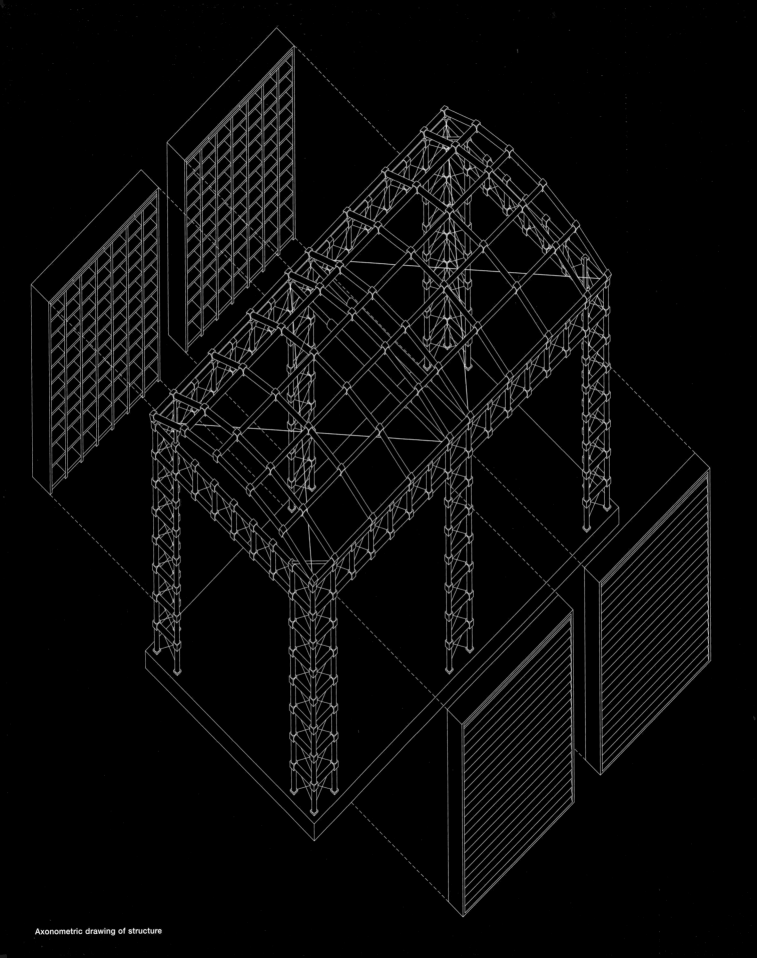

Axonometric drawing of structure

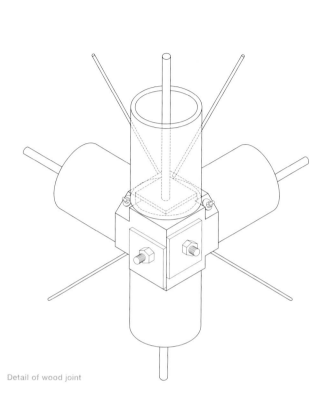

Detail of wood joint

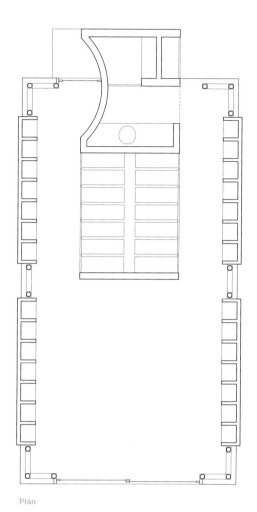

Plan

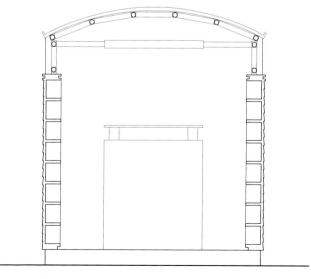

Section

View from loft

CRAVEN ROAD HOUSE

SHIM-SUTCLIFFE ARCHITECTS

Toronto, Ontario, Canada
Completed 1996

In this live-work residence in the east end of the city, Shim-Sutcliffe Architects fuses two iconic Toronto building types – the cottage and the loft. The cottage traditionally has clapboard wood siding and intimate spaces, whereas the industrial loft has high ceilings, generous lighting and an open plan. Here, the lower floor is more intimate and cottage-like, and the second level is open, airy and light-filled.

The private library is built into the large open space on the second floor, where the client can read, work and relax. Built-in bookcases on two walls contain his extensive collection of books, and a comfortable seating area set into a bay with generous windows allows for reading by natural light.

(Note: In 2006, an additional studio building was added to the site, to increase the space available for study and storage, and to display the client's collection of architectural posters.)

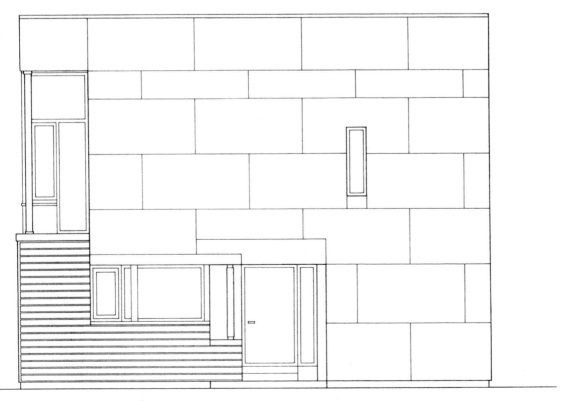

South elevation

Library interior, looking west

Craven Road House, exterior, winter, with view into library

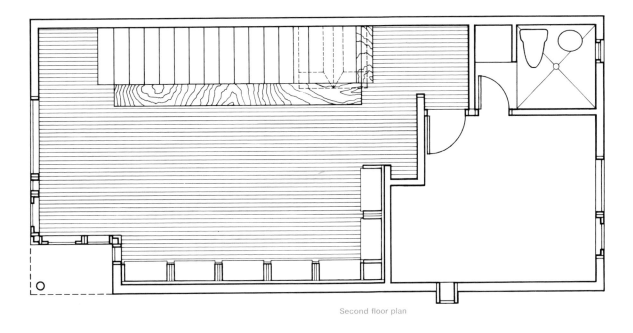

Second floor plan

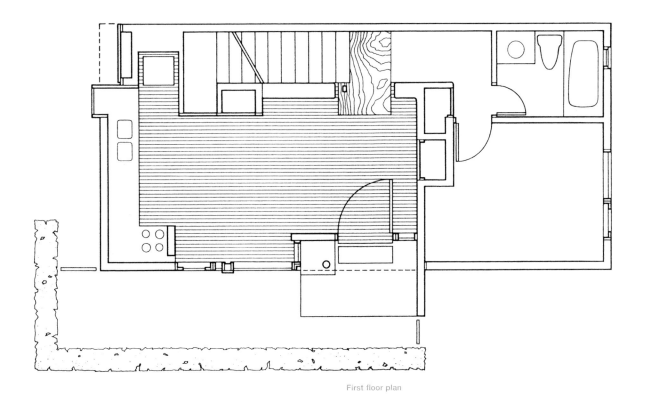

First floor plan

THE FORTSAS BIBLIOHOAX
(A TRUE STORY)

In 1840, book collectors across Europe received a very strange auction catalogue indeed. According to the catalogue, the private library of the Count of Fortsas was being sold by his heirs, who cared nothing for books, let alone the oddball nature of the Count's collection. His peculiar passion was limited to books of which only one copy was known to exist, making his relatively small but utterly unique library priceless in the eyes of similarly impassioned collectors.

On August 10, 1840, book collectors arrived in Binche, Belgium for the alleged auction, only to discover notices posted around town informing readers that the public library of Binche had bought the Count's entire library. Those collectors who didn't immediately return home in deep disappointment soon discovered that Binche did not in fact have a public library, nor had a Count of Fortsas ever counted among the town's residents. The elaborate hoax had been cooked up by a mischievous local antiquarian, who wanted to have fun with Europe's most obsessive bibliophiles. The catalogue of this fictitious sale of fictitious books is now itself a collector's item.[1]

1. With thanks to Alex Boese, who wrote a short article on the Fortsas Bibliohoax at
   www.museumofhoaxes.com/fortsas.html

CATALOGUE

D'UNE TRÈS-RICHE MAIS PEU NOMBREUSE COLLECTION

DE LIVRES

PROVENANT DE LA BIBLIOTHÈQUE

de feu M.ʳ le Comte J.-N.-A. DE FORTSAS,

dont la vente se fera à Binche, le 10 août 1840, à onze heures du matin, en l'étude et par le ministère de M.ᵉ MOURLON, Notaire, rue de l'Église, n.º 9.

Ce catalogue d'une bibliothèque qui n'a jamais existé, est une curieuse mysti-fication de M.ʳ Chalon, membre de la société des biblio-philes de Mons.

MONS.

TYPOGRAPHIE D'EM. HOYOIS, LIBRAIRE.

Prix : **50 Centimes.**

THE HOUSE OF PAPER

CARLOS MARIA DOMINGUEZ

An excerpt

From *The House of Paper,* pp. 70-73, published by Harcourt, Inc. Reprinted by permission of Harcourt, Inc.
Also available as *The Paper House,* published by Harvill. Reprinted by permission of The Random House Group Ltd.

Brauer told his labourer to build the supports for the windows and two doors on the sand. He got him to build a stone wall, and a chimney. Once the chimney was built at the side of the shack, and the door and window frames completed, he asked him to put in a cement floor. And on that floor – you can imagine the horror that fills me as I say this – he told him to turn his books into bricks…

Yes, that's right. The labourer looked on with a mixture of pity and indifference as he began to choose from the mountain of books the cart had tipped onto the clean white sand, those he wanted to protect from the wind, the rain, the rigors of winter. He had long since forgotten any idea of friendship or enmity between authors, the affinities or contradictions between Spinoza, the botany of the Amazon, and Virgil's *Aeneid;* or any concern for fine or mediocre bindings, whether they had engravings or plates, were uncut or even incunables. All he worried about was their size, their thickness, how resistant their covers might be to lime, cement and sand. The labourer squared off one of the volumes of an encyclopaedia in the corner angle, then used a string to line the others up to make a straight wall….

In a week the labourer raised, page by page, volume by volume, edition by edition, the walls of this hut on the sands of Rocha; Carlos Brauer's life's work disappeared under the cement. One work destroyed inside another. Not just sealed up. Demolished in cement….

I heard he lived there for a while, and that the cardboard, pasteboard, and paper, bound and welded into the mortar, proved more resistant than anyone could have imagined. Of course, they could not bear the weight of the roof, but the four corner posts did that. They did support their own weight, stay intact, and keep out the weather. Maybe you've seen how cement blocks crumble, how bricks can split. But the bookbindings were stronger.

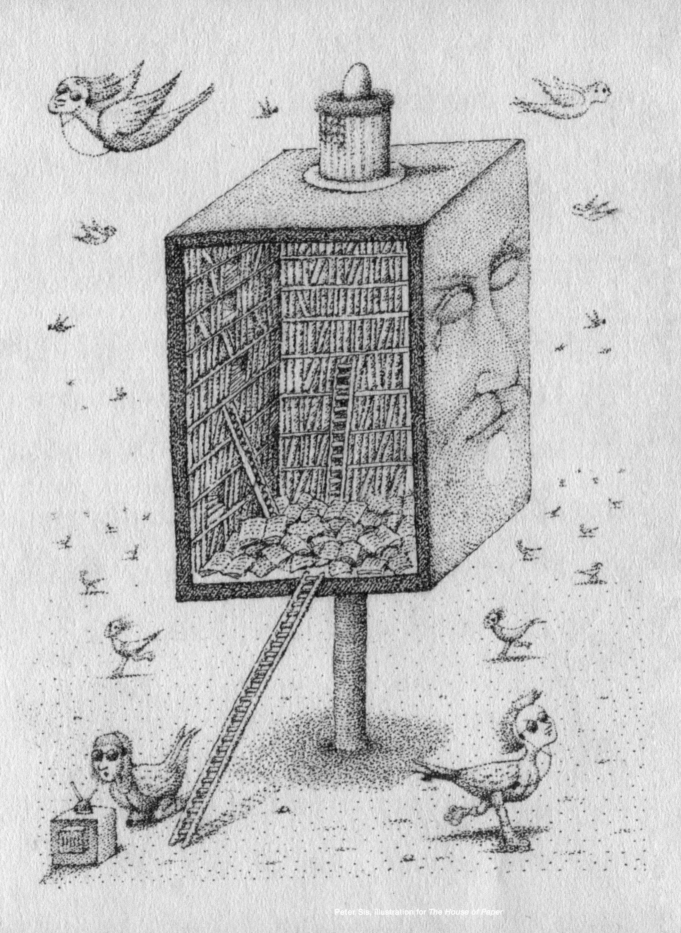

ANIMAL OBJECT #6

MICHAEL LEWIS

Toronto, 2006

Animal Object #6 is from a recent series of paintings titled *Ancestor Corridor* by Toronto artist Michael Lewis. The series imagines a large private house with different rooms, including a library/study. We know nothing about the occupant(s), and are left to guess based on clues the artist paints for us.

According to Lewis, these works explore "the connection between constructed architectural spaces and the bodies passing through them. Questions are posed such as how time affects our relationship to place; how history and memory reassign meaning over intended functionality. The paintings articulate the language of space from within, entering a shifting meaning beyond the façade. The viewer is witness to rooms and landscapes that have a consigned vantage point. The places pictured in the works reveal more about the fictions of a space than their original purpose or use, moving past representations of the actual into the realm of symbol and sign."

Michael Lewis, *Animal Object #6.* 2006, oil on canvas

SCHOOL SPIRIT

DOUGLAS COUPLAND

Vancouver, 2004

Although Douglas Coupland is known to many people primarily as a writer, he is also an accomplished visual artist. A number of his visual works relate to books and publishing.

For his vitrine diptych, *School Spirit,* Coupland took French and English language versions of a book he collaborated on with French conceptual artist, Pierre Huyghe, and chewed them up, page by page, reducing them to a pulp that he then reformed into bees' nests.

Coupland describes his work as "a strange and eerily evocative way of removing the books from cultural time and relocating them in evolutionary or even geological time." According to the artist, *School Spirit* "foregrounds

the artificiality and transience of human culture, while challenging the notion of the book as a cultural format being beyond introspection or reevaluation. It also exposes viewers to the relative crudeness of bookmaking, and leads them closer to the notion that within a few hundred years, books will most likely be viewed as a transitional gateway technology that was required along the way to the creation of an all-digital universe."

Douglas Coupland, *School Spirit*. 2004, chewed up books on metal rods, twigs

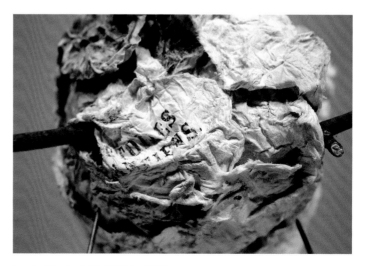

Douglas Coupland, detail of *School Spirit*

FUTURE

"*Mary Kay is one of the secret masters of the world: a librarian. They control information. Don't ever piss one off.*"

SPIDER ROBINSON ~ *The Callahan Touch*

111

THE FUTURE OF THE LIBRARY

Portrait of Callimachus. 16ᵗʰ Century woodcut by
Tobias Stimmer, after P. Giovio, *Elonga virorum literis
illustrium*, (P. Perna: Basel, 1577)

At the centre of every well-run library is a host of librarians. Librarians are information professionals trained in library and information science. They are also the human face of the library. In recent years, many librarians have become highly specialized, choosing to concentrate on areas such as public service, reference and research, technical service, collections development, archives, systems, electronic resources or school library media.

Historically, librarians have been masters of the most advanced information technology, frequently at the forefront of developments. Callimachus, the grammarian and poet who was among the most famous scholars to be employed by the Ancient Library of Alexandria, developed the West's first cataloguing system, known as the *pinakes*. This was a collection of scrolls that listed all the works held in the library, divided into categories and then further sub-divided by title and author. Since then, librarians have worked to develop an impressive array of cataloguing systems and library software, plus the MARC standards for cataloguing records electronically. Librarians have also played a large role in teaching the public how to navigate these sophisticated systems and how to move to more virtual working environments.

Admittedly, since anyone can Google anything or post information on the Internet nowadays, modern technology is sometimes said to render the role of the librarian obsolete. Nothing could be further from the truth. Librarians determine the scholarly validity and accuracy of electronic reference material, and teach their patrons how to conduct in-depth research that goes well beyond the snippets of information available through search engines. Furthermore, most librarians are remarkably well-informed about the information-sharing possibilities of the latest technological advances, including the open source movement, podcasting, voice-recognition software and the advanced 3D virtual libraries in Second Life.

It was, in fact, a group of librarians, led by Canadian Kitty Pope at the Alliance Library System in East Peoria, Illinois, that created the hugely popular Alliance Second Life Library, an online interactive research and learning environment. Librarians are also busily digitizing vast collections, from Project Gutenberg to Librivox, an online source of audiobooks, in order to make their collections even more accessible. With advances in technology, the image of the librarian has likewise evolved, something that technology writer and broadcaster Nora Young investigates in the following pages.

One key question remains – now that people can access information from practically anywhere through computers and cellphones, *will libraries as built forms cease to matter and disappear?* Hardly. The library as a human institution is far too important to vanish into cyberspace. The need for collective experience and social interaction will never go away, which is why new libraries continue to be built, and existing libraries are being expanded to meet ever-growing demand. New technologies have not necessarily cancelled out the old ones; they build on them or add another layer of sophistication to existing systems. This provides the library patron with more opportunities and points of access. Besides, the sensorial experience of reading a book holds too great an allure. So, despite the hype, the printed book will not disappear anytime soon.

We close *Logotopia* with a work by artist Adam David Brown. *Index* utilizes the iconic *Oxford English Dictionary* as a built form, borrows the technology of the geological core sample and combines the two with light and projection to create a thought provoking meditation on changing technology and the library through time.

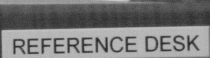

Action figure of librarian Nancy Pearl

OPPOSITES ATTRACT:
CHANGING TECHNOLOGY AND THE
LIBRARIAN IN POPULAR CULTURE
NORA YOUNG

Oracle, Cover image from *Birds of Prey*
(DC Comics, New Edition, 2002)

If you remember Barbara Gordon from the 1960s TV series *Batman,* you have a very different picture of her than those who have continued to follow her more recent adventures in comic books. On TV, Barbara was the bookish daughter of Commissioner Gordon, and worked in the Gotham Public Library. A classic "Marian the Librarian", she wore heavy glasses, plain clothes, and seemed to yearn for Bruce Wayne with repressed longing. It was only as the superhero, Batgirl, that she emerged from her shell to become a red-haired, sexy spitfire.

Meanwhile, in the comic book world, after a shooting left her paralyzed from the waist down, Barbara Gordon went on to re-emerge in 1989 as Oracle: a whip-smart hacker and computer expert who helps superheroes by using her computer savvy… and her library skills!

Barbara's move from Batgirl to Oracle offers a neat summary of the way our relationship to information has changed. As the information economy has grown, computers, the Web, and the manipulation of information have become surprisingly sexy, at least when compared to the culture of the book. Information and its management have always been important, they just haven't always been *hot.*

Librarians have been stock characters in pop culture for decades; they are frequently sources of comedy, often made out to be faintly ridiculous, or painfully out of touch with the everyday emotions and priorities of the "regular people" who visit the library; they are even occasionally made out to be menacing. The stereotypes of librarians are more than pop culture fun, however; they are a way of understanding our relationship to information, and how that relationship is changing in contemporary Internet culture.[1]

Many of us feel quite conflicted about formal or "book" knowledge; we are aware of its power, but anxious about our abilities to manipulate and understand it. We know it's a key to financial and social status, not to mention self-knowledge, yet we fear that we just aren't smart enough to use it. Librarians' facility in searching for information, and their role as the access point for information, makes them a lightning rod for these contradictory anxieties and desires. In surveying the online literature about librarian archetypes, what stands out for me is the way they flip-flop between polar opposites. Whether the archetype addresses power, sexuality, or sociability, a personality type and its complete opposite are both equally represented. I'd argue this is an expression of the complex feelings that learning, books and information call up in us, and that it's an attempt to manage those contradictory feelings, mostly through humour.

As Adriane Allen suggests in an online essay[2], the librarian with an alter ego is a strong convention in pop culture, making it the clearest example of how this duality occurs; the opposites turn up within the same character, turning the librarian into a kind of double agent. Consider *The Spy Who Came in From the Cold*[3], the 1965 movie starring Richard Burton. He is literally a double agent who has been given a cover job as a library assistant. It's the perfect, meek cover for a spy. Yet it's also true that librarians have a lot in common with spies, detectives and the like. Neither is required to know a lot about subjects as much as to know how to *find out* a lot about subjects, and to know their way around an information system.

---

1. As might be expected when the subject is the librarian, there are many resources describing and offering taxonomies of librarians in popular culture, including many websites affiliated with university Library Sciences programs. I am indebted to these sites for providing me with lists and examples of librarians in pop culture. Please refer to references at the end of this essay.
2. "The Librarian With an Alter Ego Convention" appears as part of a content analysis of libraries in mass media. See the essay at http://besser.tsoa.nyu.edu/impact/f01/Focus/Image/index.htm
3. Daniel Gwyn looks at librarians and spies in an essay online through McGill's Library Sciences program, focusing on Nathan the spy librarian in the *Once a Thief* TV show; intriguingly, this librarian sees the world almost entirely in terms of conspiracy theories: the secretive librarian seeing the world in terms of secrets! http://www.gslis.mcgill.ca/marginal/mar7-3/The%20Fictional%20Librarian%20Part%202.htm

Poster commissioned by the American Library Association in partnership with DC Comics, 2004 (opposite page)

Stereotype of stern, repressed librarian

This "double agent" character suggests a broader cliché of the librarian as secretive. The satirical TV show, *The Colbert Report*, recently joked about this during an interview by flashing the words "librarians are hiding something" on-screen. Perhaps this is because the librarian does not reveal her/himself to us. They know the questions we have, the books we choose, but what do we know of theirs?

A more positive take on this secrecy is the image of the librarian as a guardian of information with the power to instruct the uninitiated in arcane mysteries, a sort of Yoda of the book. Think of Rupert Giles, the school librarian in the *Buffy the Vampire Slayer* series, who provides access and interprets the secret knowledge contained in all those dusty old tomes. The librarian in this scenario may be the guardian of a whole culture. In the dystopian world of *Soylent Green,* the 1973 science fiction film, for instance, books are no longer published and most people don't read. Librarian/researchers are referred to as "books", vessels to carry the knowledge of the culture. The librarian may even be the guardian of the planet, as seen in the recent comic book series *Rex Libris,* in which our hunky bespectacled hero does battle with largely illiterate intergalactic villains.

The guardian figure has its sinister opposite, too: the librarian as withholder of information, barring the way to knowledge. This is grounded in a complex sentiment. There's a strong cultural pull around the idea of books as the source of power, but also as a source of danger, of holding more information than the reader is able to handle; the librarian who can grant or deny that knowledge is a powerful figure. A frequently cited pop cultural example is Malachi, the head librarian in the enormous monastery library in the book and movie *The Name of the Rose.* Malachi zealously guards over which books monks ought to see and which they ought not to.

A further doubling occurs around sexuality and the female librarian. That the repressed librarian is so often a stereotype, I think speaks to (male) discomfort with women's relationship to knowledge. Desexualizing the librarian makes her an object of pity and mockery. Margaret Atwood presents a darkly feminist take on this is in her novel *The Handmaid's Tale,* in which the main character, who used to be a librarian, is reduced to sex slavery. This archetype, too, contains its opposite: the librarian as sex-crazed vixen, where the repression is a thin veneer waiting to be broken through. This speaks to yet another duality in our feelings about knowledge, that one cannot be simultaneously cerebral and sensual.

Most commonly, there's the stern, controlling librarian, almost always an elderly woman. She surely reflects our sense of hierarchy around knowledge, a hierarchy that extends beyond the library to the workplace and school. The flip side of this hierarchical cliché is the librarian as timid mouse. The meek librarian has thus been disempowered in every sense except his or her control of knowledge: socially awkward, unpopular and unattractive, thus completely lacking in all other forms of social power. This cliché also feeds into the popular myth that bookish people, or "nerds", don't have friends, and that it's therefore best not to appear too smart.

Should a gentleman offer a Tiparillo to a librarian?

She'll read anything she can get her hands on. From Medieval History to How-To-Build-a-24-Foot-Iceboat. Loves books. Loves new ideas.

Okay. No doubt, she's seen the unusual, slim Tiparillo shape.

She's been intrigued by the neat, white tip. She may even know that there are two Tiparillos. Regular, for a mild smoke. And new Tiparillo M with menthol, for a cold smoke.

Your only problem is which to offer. P.S. If she accepts your Tiparillo,* remember to fumble with the matches until she decides to light it herself.

That way, she'll have to put down the book.

JUST BECAUSE I'M A LIBRARIAN DOESN'T MEAN I'M AT ALL TAME.

BUCKO.

Excerpt from *Rex Libris*, Vol. 1, Issue 1

If these are some of the common stereotypes of the librarian in book culture, how do they stand up in today's information economy? Though librarians still turn up in pop culture, they aren't the stock comedic figures they used to be. Characters in movies who want information, after all, are more likely to look it up on the computer than go to the library. You could argue that everyone who uses the Internet is a librarian. We all sift through multiple websites, looking for the most accurate or entertaining material. Those of us who have social networking profiles are not only content creators, but also managers of information systems, choosing what information is available and who can have access to it.

It would be a mistake, though, to suggest that the information economy has given us a purely democratic, un-conflicted relationship to knowledge. There is enormous variation in people's skills at accessing and understanding information online. For many people, digital culture is still a huge source of anxiety. So, it's no surprise that the librarian is largely being replaced in our pop culture iconography by the hacker and the computer geek. This is the person who now inhabits the polar dualities as the locus of our hopes and anxieties about information. The hacker is seen as good and evil, sexy and a loner, a geek and a powerhouse, and for a lot of the same reasons.[4]

Intriguingly, librarians are increasingly using new tools of social media to help library users access and use digital information more effectively. We're seeing more and more librarian podcasts, for instance, as well as librarian bloggers and librarian-based groups on social networks such as Facebook. It is both a means to reach out to communities of potential library customers, and a way of connecting with colleagues. One of the most interesting experiments in this regard is in Second Life (SL), the hugely popular 3D virtual landscape that users navigate via avatars, or cartoon representations of themselves. More and more libraries are developing a presence in Second Life, including at dedicated library landscapes such as Cybrary City or Alliance Second Life Library. Real world librarians create avatars that staff virtual libraries, helping visitors with reference questions and queries about Second Life itself. According to Jim Milles, a professor and Director of the Charles B. Sears Law Library at the University at Buffalo, and an SL librarian, while his library's real world users may not be SL residents yet, it's at least possible that "SL, or something like it – immersive, interactive online 3D environments – represent the future."

The potential in the future is for librarians to extend the notion of the library community online, and to offer a truly welcoming point of access to information for other community members. Right now, it's a great way for librarians to connect with other progressive librarians. As Milles describes its appeal to him, "SL provides a uniquely involving way to meet and interact with people from all over the world – because it's not the technology, it's the people that are important in SL."

At the moment, people who use Second Life are likely already pretty tech savvy. The potential for participatory social media tools such as Second Life, though, is that librarians can use them to break down that long-standing ambivalence and anxiety about the relationship among user, librarian and information. How appropriate that the librarian, pop cultural double, should create a double – an avatar – to do so.

Of the numerous online surveys of librarians and popular culture, these are the ones I found most helpful.

Antoinette Graham maintains an extensive list and description of libraries and librarians in the movies at: http://home.earthlink.net/~movielibrarians/#handmaid

Another helpful site for librarians in film was created by Martin Raish at Brigham Young University: http://emp.byui.edu/raishm/films/introduction.html

A great overview of librarians in pop culture is *Spectacles: How Pop Culture Views Librarians*, by Ruth A. Kneale, from a talk given at the 2007 SLA annual conference: http://www.librarian-image.net/img07/

For the discussion of the theme of librarians with alter egos, please see: http://besser.tsoa.nyu.edu/impact/f01/Focus/Image/index.htm

Kristi Mulhern at the University of British Columbia prepared this helpful overview of librarians in popular culture: http://www.slais.ubc.ca/courses/libr500/03-04 wt1/assignments/www/K Mulhern/index.htm

4. Consider such diverse examples as nerdy Marshall in the TV series *Alias* vs. the ubercool hackers in *The Matrix* trilogy.

Front cover of *Rex Libris,* Vol. 1, Issue 1 (opposite page)

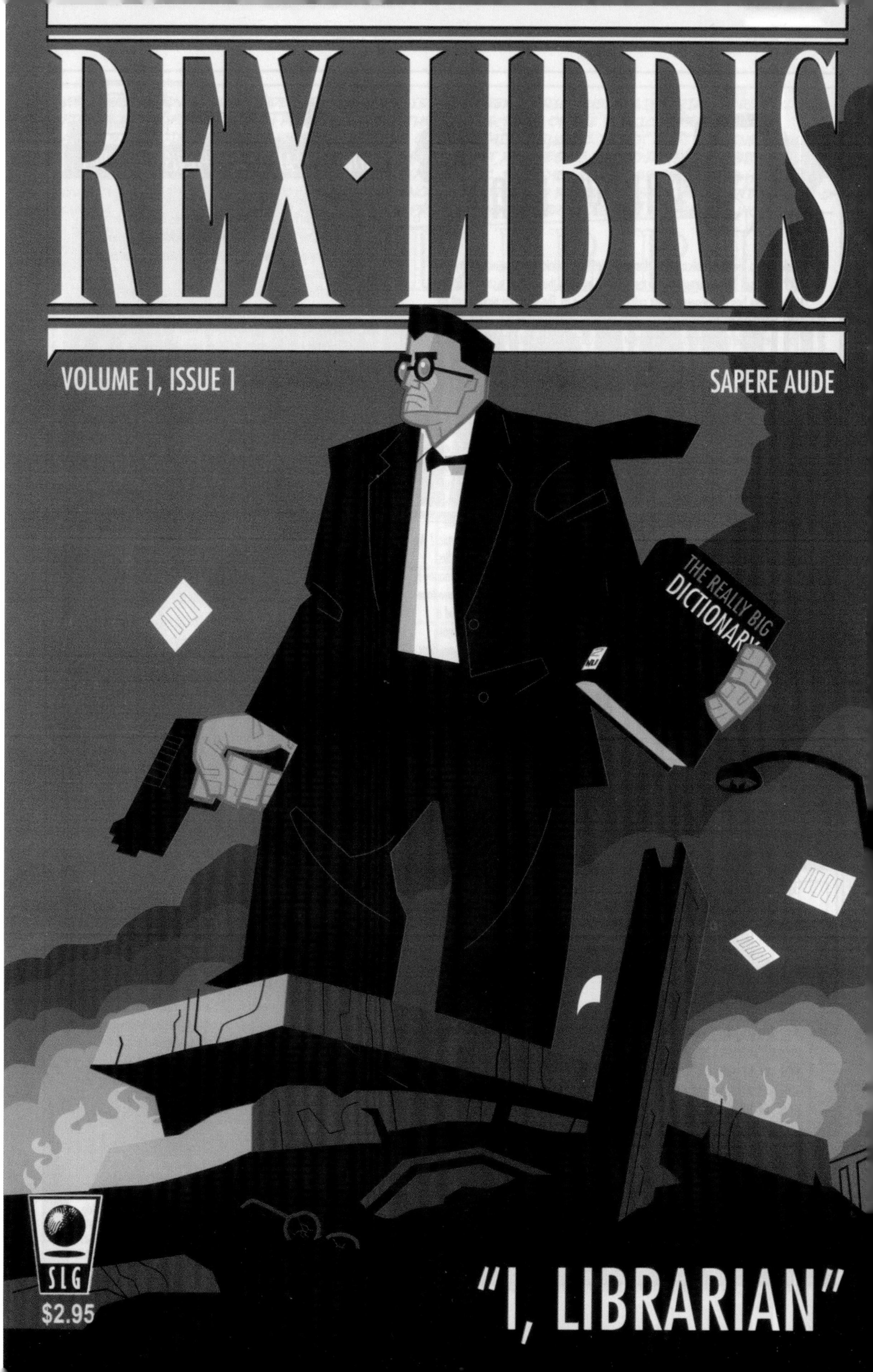
REX·LIBRIS
VOLUME 1, ISSUE 1
SAPERE AUDE
THE REALLY BIG
DICTIONARY
SLG
$2.95
"I, LIBRARIAN"

ALLIANCE SECOND LIFE LIBRARY

ALLIANCE LIBRARY SYSTEM
AND HUNDREDS OF VOLUNTEERS
AROUND THE WORLD

www.alliancelibrarysystem.com or www.secondlife.com
2006 – Ongoing

An interview between Sascha Hastings (SH) and Kitty Pope (KP)

The Alliance Second Life Library is a 3D virtual library that was started by the Alliance Library System in East Peoria, Illinois in April 2006. It exists in the online, interactive world of Second Life, which is populated by avatars – cartoon digital representations of real people who control their avatars from their computers. The Alliance Second Life Library was started by a Canadian – Kitty Pope – who is also the Executive Director of the Alliance Library System. Curator Sascha Hastings reached her at her office in East Peoria in June 2007.

SH: Can you tell me about the early days of the Alliance Second Life Library?

KP: At first, we just rented a small building in Second Life and simply asked the question, do avatars want a library? Within three months we had 200 librarians from around the world who wanted to volunteer to help us out, because initially there were only two of us who were looking after the Second Life Library. So then we built one big central reference library. And then we built another, and then we added an island. And now, two years later, we have 52 libraries spread across what we call the Information Archipelago. We have general reference libraries, but also libraries that deal with specific genres or subjects, such as a library for Alzheimer's patients, and we have academic libraries. The academic community has taken Second Life on like gangbusters because they think this is the new frontier when it comes to adult education, since you can give students an immersive experience from the comfort of their own home. For example, community colleges in British Columbia and Ontario have been very active in Second Life since day one and are already teaching courses in Second Life about Second Life.

SH: What do Alliance Second Life Library buildings look like?

KP: When we first started we wanted to recreate our own world in the virtual world, so we built libraries that looked in our minds like libraries should look, you know, the Carnegie look, kind of Greek and Roman with stairs going up to the circulation desk. But we learned pretty quickly that because avatars can fly and move, and because the weather is beautiful all the time in Second Life, we don't need walls, and so the architecture has changed significantly in the last year and a half, moving from a real bricks and mortar visualization to a truly open-air or glass look, with landing platforms where avatars can teleport in, and minimal furniture so it's easy for them to move around – a kind of style that really speaks to the 21st century.

SH: Were architects involved?

KP: Our first architect was a summer student who was also an architecture student, and we asked him what a medical library might look like in Second Life. So he started to play around and incorporated a stethoscope wrapped around the ceiling of a sort of flat building that was very Frank Lloyd Wright-esque. For the other buildings, sometimes librarians build them, but they tend to be by people who specialize in building in Second Life.

Kitty Pope with her avatar, "The Library Goddess"

SH: How do you build in Second Life?

KP: You have a platform on which you put digital pieces of structure. The simplest thing is to have a box-like prefab house that you buy with the Linden dollar, which is the Second Life currency. Or you can actually start from scratch and design your own building to your own specifications with your own structural elements. We deal in what we call "prims" – short for "primitives" – which are like building blocks within the virtual world that you can shrink or stretch or shape as you like and then construct your building out of them.

SH: How does the way people use the Alliance Second Life Library compare to how they use real life libraries?

KP: I've found much to my delight that avatars are even more inquisitive than you or me. They love to ask questions, they love to go to events, and they love to interact with other people. For example, last Hallowe'en, we had Stephen King live, on stage, reading and talking about his books. His avatar was on stage, and an audience of avatars from all around the world was listening and asking questions about why he wrote this and not this, or if he worries about the scare factor in his books, or how he compares his books to the

movie versions, and all kinds of other questions. And I was sitting next to a librarian from the Netherlands!

People also come to the Second Life Library to ask reference questions – about one third are traditional library reference questions. Another third are health related, which is just like a regular public library. And one third are about Second Life. Can you guess what the most popular question we get asked is?

SH: Umm... How can I borrow a book?

KP: No... it's "Can you teach me how to fly?" And so our 400 volunteers that we now have at the reference centre are regularly giving people the quick "how to fly in Second Life" lesson!

SH: Can you actually borrow a book ?

KP: You can read a digital book but you can't get a printed copy. We do have quite a few digitized books at this point though. And the next level for us is to connect with some of the big digitized collections so that people can also access them through Second Life.

SH: What else is coming up for the Alliance Second Life Library?

KP: I think the next step is going to be more virtual worlds. For example, at this point we have learning environments like the Renaissance Island, where

you can walk down a street and hear people speaking in Old English or go into a shop and talk to a shopkeeper. At the end of one of the streets is the Globe Theatre, and so if you're an English or Drama teacher you can stand on the stage with your class and read *Othello* – in the Globe Theatre. That was our first real exploration of an immersive environment and we're looking at many more. For example, the 200th anniversary of the Lincoln Debates is coming up, and in America these are huge, so we'll likely be doing an immersive world about Lincoln. We're also hoping to do an immersive environment about the music of North America from 1900 to 2000. The other thing is, right now, when I say you "talk" in Second Life, you actually do it by typing, which is a little slow, and we've recognized that for some time now. But we've been doing prototypes on voice recognition, and we think that within another six months, we'll be fully auditory. I think Second Life really is the ultimate way to learn because it's an immersive environment that truly combines all the senses into a learning experience that goes beyond the classroom.

A selection of screen captures from events on different islands in the Alliance Second Life Library's Information Archipelago

INDEX
ADAM DAVID BROWN

Toronto, 2006

The *Oxford English Dictionary* is like other dictionaries in that it represents a kind of universal library of words.

But it is unlike other English dictionaries in that it attempts to provide a biography for each word. The words are traced back to their earliest written sources, usually dating back to antiquity. The history of the English language is that it expanded by colonizing and appropriating many other languages from around the globe. *Index* cross-references the *OED* with the notion of a geological core sample, which alters the architecture of the dictionary and makes it strange. *Index* looks at language in geological terms as though the dictionary was the source of meaning. The result is a conceptual transgression that ruptures the empirical function of the dictionary and repositions it as an object under investigation.

Adam David Brown, *Index*, 2006, *Oxford English Dictionary* (modified), video projection, table

CONTRIBUTORS

Shigeru Ban is an architect born in Tokyo in 1957. He is particularly known for his innovative use of organic materials such as paper, bamboo and engineered wood. Library of a Poet in Kanagawa, Japan was Ban's first permanent building made of paper tubes. He is currently working on the Centre Pompidou Metz in France.

Lise Bissonnette is President and Chief Executive Officer of Bibliothèque et Archives nationales du Québec. Prior to her appointment, Mme. Bissonnette served for eight years as publisher and editor of the daily *Le Devoir*. She is the author of eight books – three collections of essays and five works of fiction.

Ray Bradbury is the acclaimed author of more than thirty books. Among the best known are *The Martian Chronicles, Fahrenheit 451* and *Something Wicked This Way Comes.* He lives in Los Angeles and his latest work is *Now and Forever* (HarperCollins, 2008).

Adam David Brown is an artist living in Toronto. A graduate of the Ontario College of Art and Design, he completed his Master of Fine Arts at the University of Guelph. Adam has exhibited work in Canada, Europe and the United States.

Dr. Saad Eskander has been Director of the Iraq National Library and Archive (INLA) in Baghdad since 2003. From November 2006 until July 2007 he wrote a blog about his experiences at the INLA, which is posted on the website of the British Library at http://www.bl.uk/iraqdiary.html.

Denis Farley lives and works in Montréal. He has exhibited in many galleries in Québec, Canada, Europe and the United States. He is represented in public and private collections, including Musée d'art Contemporain de Montréal, Fonds National d'Art Contemporain à Paris and the Canadian Museum of Contemporary Photography. Farley is represented by Galerie Graff in Montréal.

Hariri Pontarini Architects is a Toronto-based architectural practice which draws on the collective skills and expertise of over 40 registered and intern architects, and support staff. Principals Siamak Hariri and David Pontarini have been partners in practice since 1994, and maintain shared values about responsive, high quality design and architecture that has a strong sense of place and a demonstrated significance in materiality.

Kongats Architects Inc. was founded in Toronto in 1990. Since then, its work has consisted primarily of cultural and educational projects. Alar Kongats has received several awards, including a Governor General's Medal in Architecture for the Centennial College Student Centre. Major current projects include a new Student Centre for Nipissing University and Canadore College in North Bay, and a new Medical School for the University of Toronto at Mississauga.

Guy Laramée is a Montréal-based interdisciplinary artist who has worked in visual arts, theatre, music and literature. He has received numerous grants and awards, and has collaborated with Robert Lepage (Québec), Volker Hesse (Zurich), Rachel Rosenthal (Los Angeles) and Larry Tremblay (Montréal). His work has been seen and heard across North America, Latin America, Europe and Japan.

Michael Lewis has exhibited extensively throughout Canada. LandymoreKeith Contemporary Art represents his work. His paintings are held in the public collection of the Art Gallery of Ontario and in international private collections. He studied at the Ontario College of Art and lives and works in Toronto.

Alberto Manguel is a Canadian writer, editor and public intellectual who was born in Buenos Aires, Argentina in 1948. He has received numerous international awards and honours and is the author of many works of fiction and non-fiction, including *The Library at Night, With Borges* and *A History of Reading.*

Patkau Architects is an internationally recognized architectural design studio based in Vancouver. There are currently three principals: John Patkau, Patricia Patkau and Michael Cunningham, and three associates: David Shone, Peter Suter and Greg Boothroyd. The firm seeks to explore the full richness and diversity of architectural practice, understanding it as a critical cultural act that engages their most fundamental desires and aspirations.

Kitty Pope was born and raised in Canada, and is now Executive Director of the Alliance Library System in East Peoria, Illinois. She has been at the forefront of developing the Alliance Second Life Library, which won The ALA/Information Today Inc. Library of the Future Award in June 2007. Pope is also a frequent lecturer on the virtual world of Second Life.

Shim-Sutcliffe Architects of Toronto is an architectural practice interested in the integration of furniture, architecture and landscape. Shim-Sutcliffe's built architectural work has been honoured with eight Governor General's Medals and Awards for Architecture along with American Institute of Architects, American Wood Council, Canadian Wood Council, *Architectural Record Interiors* and the *I.D. Magazine* Design Review awards.

Snøhetta AS was formed in 1989 in Norway. Today, its offices in Oslo and New York employ 80 architects and designers. It is best known for the Bibliotheca Alexandrina, the New National Opera in Oslo and the World Trade Centre Museum in New York. Snøhetta has won numerous international awards, including the Aga Khan Prize in 2004, and has developed a reputation for maintaining a strong relationship between landscape and architecture in its projects.

Robert Jan van Pelt teaches in the School of Architecture at the University of Waterloo. He has published widely on the history of architecture, Holocaust history and Auschwitz and has engaged in the battle against Holocaust denial. His personal library serves as a refuge from all of that.

Nora Young is a Toronto-based writer and broadcaster. She pursues her fascination with technology and culture on public radio, on television, in print and online. She was the founding host of CBC Radio's *Definitely Not The Opera* and the technology show, *Spark,* and is the technology columnist for CBC radio afternoon shows.

IMAGE SOURCES

PAGE 2: Fol. 15 from: Millard Meiss and Elizabeth H. Beatson, *The Belles Heures of Jean, Duke of Berry.* (New York: George Braziller, 1974) p. 4. Reprinted by permission.

PAGE 4: Collection of Robert Jan van Pelt.

PAGE 12: Photo: Gerald Zugmann/Snøhetta Architects.

PAGE 13: Top image: From: Hermann Goell, *Die Weisen und Gelehrten des Alterthums*, 2nd edition. (Leipzig: Otto Spamer, 1876) p.139. Photo: akg-images. Bottom image: Photo: James Willis.

PAGE 14: Top image: Naples, Galleria Naz. di Capodimonte. Photo: akg-images/Electa. Bottom image: Carl Sagan, *Cosmos.* (New York and Canada: Random House, 1980) p.21. Reprinted by permission of the Estate of Carl Sagan.

PAGE 15: From: *Hermann Goell, Die Weisen und Gelehrten des Alterthums*, 2nd edition. (Leipzig: Otto Spamer, 1876) p.359. Photo: akg-images.

PAGE 16: Conrad Gesner, *Bibliotheca Universalis und Appendix.* (Osnabrueck: Otto Zeller Verlagsbuckhandlung, 1966). Facsimile of the 1545 original. Collection of Robert Jan van Pelt.

PAGE 17: Top image: Copper engraving published in: Johannes van Meurs, *Illustrum Hollandiae & Westfrisiae ordinum alma Academiae Leidensis* (Leiden: Jacobus Marcus and Justus à Colster, 1614) p. 228. Bottom image: Courtesy of Herzog August Bibliothek Wolfenbüttel. Reprinted by permission.

PAGE 18: Courtesy of Herzog August Bibliothek Wolfenbüttel. Reprinted by permission.

PAGE 19: From: Hjalmar H. Boyesen, *The Works of Goethe*, Vol. II. (George Barrie: Philadelphia, 1885), unnumbered plate. Collection of Robert Jan van Pelt.

PAGE 20: http://www.gutenberg.org

PAGE 21: http://www.cmu.edu

PAGE 22: Collection of Robert Jan van Pelt. Reprinted by permission. ©Erik Desmazières/SODRAC (1997).

PAGE 23: Collection of Robert Jan van Pelt. Reprinted by permission. ©Erik Desmazières/SODRAC (1997).

PAGE 24-25: Collection of Robert Jan van Pelt. Reprinted by permission. ©Erik Desmazières/SODRAC (1997).

PAGE 26: Courtesy of Snøhetta Architects.

PAGE 27: Photo: James Willis.

PAGE 28: Photo: James Willis.

PAGE 29: Courtesy of Snøhetta Architects.

PAGE 30: Photos: James Willis. Plans: Courtesy of Snøhetta Architects.

PAGE 31: Photo: James Willis.

PAGE 33: Photo: David Popplow.

PAGE 36: Courtesy of British Library, BL Ref.#A683 P.P 7611 volume 30, p. 430. Reprinted by permission.

PAGE 37: Top image: From: *Allgemeine Familien-Zeitung*, Yr. 1, No. 5, (H. Schoenlein: Stuttgart, 1869) p.72/73. Photo: akg-images. Bottom image: Photo: Georges Fessy. Courtesy of Dominique Perrault Architecte.

PAGE 38: Photo: James Dow.

PAGE 39: Photo: James Dow.

PAGE 40: Photo: Bernard Fougères/Bibliothèque nationale du Québec.

PAGE 41: Photo: James Dow.

PAGE 42: Photos: James Dow.

PAGE 43: Courtesy of Patkau Architects.

PAGE 44-45: Photo: James Dow.

PAGE 46: Photo: James Dow.

PAGE 47: Courtesy of Patkau Architects.

PAGE 48: Photos: James Dow.

PAGE 49: Courtesy of Patkau Architects.

PAGE 50: Photo: Bernard Fougères/Bibliothèque nationale du Québec.

PAGE 51: Courtesy of Patkau Architects.

PAGE 53: Photos courtesy of the artist.

PAGE 55: http://www.iraqnla.org. Reprinted by permission.

PAGE 58: Archives of Ontario, S-2063. Reprinted by permission.

PAGE 59: Photo: Corbis Corporation, image #VV1951.

PAGE 62-63: Source: Archives of the Corporation of the City of Cambridge. Photo: David Popplow.

PAGE 64: Photo: Ben Rahn/A-Frame Inc.

PAGE 65: Top image: Photo: Ben Rahn/A-Frame Inc. Bottom image: Photo: Steve Payne.

PAGE 66: Photo: Ben Rahn/A-Frame Inc.

PAGE 67: Photo: Ben Rahn/A-Frame Inc.

PAGE 68: Courtesy of Kongats Architects Inc.

PAGE 69: Courtesy of Kongats Architects Inc.

PAGE 70-71: Photo: Steve Payne.

PAGE 72: Courtesy of Kongats Architects Inc.

PAGE 73: Photo: Ben Rahn/A-Frame Inc.

PAGE 74: Courtesy of Hariri Pontarini Architects.

PAGE 75: Photo: Darius Himes.

PAGE 76: Photo: Darius Himes.

PAGE 77: Photo: Darius Himes.

PAGE 78: Top image: Photo: Darius Himes. Bottom image: Courtesy of Hariri Pontarini Architects.

PAGE 79: Photos: Courtesy of Hariri Pontarini Architects.

PAGE 81: Photo: Robert McNair.

PAGE 84: Purchased on eBay.

PAGE 85: Collection of Robert Jan van Pelt.

PAGE 86-87: Collection of Robert Jan van Pelt.

PAGE 88: Collection of Robert Jan van Pelt.

PAGE 89: Photo: Ana Obiols.

PAGE 90: Collection of Robert Jan van Pelt.

PAGE 91: Photo: Ana Obiols.

PAGE 92: Courtesy of Shigeru Ban Architects.

PAGE 93: Courtesy of Shigeru Ban Architects.

PAGE 94 - 95: Drawings by David Takacs, re-drawn from images provided by Shigeru Ban Architects.

PAGE 96-97: Courtesy of Shigeru Ban Architects.

PAGE 98: Courtesy of Shim-Sutcliffe Architects Inc.

PAGE 99: Photo: James Dow.

PAGE 100: Photo: R. Hill.

PAGE 101: Courtesy of Shim-Sutcliffe Architects Inc.

PAGE 103: Courtesy of University of Delaware Library.

PAGE 105: Illustration by Peter Sis. From: Carlos Maria Dominguez, *The House of Paper.* English Translation copyright ©2005 by Nick Caistor. (Harcourt: Orlando, 2005) p. 38. Reprinted by permission of Harcourt, Inc.

PAGE 107: Collection of the artist. Photo: Robert McNair.

PAGE 109: Photos: Danny Custudio/Monte Clark Gallery.

PAGE 112: 16th Century Woodcut by Tobias Stimmer, after P. Giovio, *Elonga virorum literis illustrium.* (P. Perna: Basel, 1577). Photo: akg-images.

PAGE 113: Collection of Cambridge Galleries. Photo: Robert McNair.

PAGE 114: Cover image from *Birds of Prey* (DC Comics, New Edition, 2002). Reprinted by permission.

PAGE 115: Original artwork by Gene Ha in cooperation with DC Comics. Reprinted by permission.

PAGE 117: *Playboy*, year unknown. Purchased on eBay.

PAGE 118: Excerpt from James Turner: *Rex Libris*, Vol.1, Issue 1, p.9. Reprinted by permission of the author.

PAGE 119: Front cover of James Turner: *Rex Libris*, Vol.1, Issue 1. Reprinted by permission of the author.

PAGE 121: Courtesy of the Alliance Library System.

PAGE 122-123: Courtesy of the Alliance Library System.

PAGE 125: Collection of the artist. Photo courtesy of the artist.

INSIDE BACK COVER: Back cover of James Turner: *Rex Libris*, Vol.1, Issue 1. Reprinted by permission of the author.

ACKNOWLEDGEMENTS

*Logotopia: The Library in Architecture,
Art and the Imagination*
ISBN – 10: 1897001266
ISBN – 13: 978-1897001264
Printed in Canada

CURATOR

Sascha Hastings

EDITORS

Sascha Hastings
Esther E. Shipman

TECHNICAL EDITOR

Marco Polo

DESIGN

Catalogue, Exhibition
Bhandari & Plater Inc., Toronto

COVER AND INSIDE COVER PHOTOS

Robert McNair

PUBLISHER

Cambridge Galleries
1 North Square
Cambridge, Ontario Canada N1S 2K6
(519)621-0460
www.cambridgegalleries.ca

DISTRIBUTOR

ABC Art Books Canada
372 St. Cathérine West
Montréal, Québec Canada H3B 1A2
www.abcartbookscanada.com

Cambridge Galleries Design at Riverside
acknowledges the ongoing support of:

The Corporation of the City of Cambridge
Ontario Arts Council
Canada Council for the Arts
The University of Waterloo School of Architecture

The Curator wishes to further acknowledge:

Robert Jan van Pelt of the University of Waterloo
School of Architecture for his substantial
contribution of materials to both the *Logotopia*
exhibit and publication.

Esther E. Shipman, Curator of Architecture
and Design, Cambridge Galleries for her editorial
insights and supervision, and her collaboration
on the exhibition.

Marco Polo of the Ryerson University
Department of Architectural Science for his
attention to technical detail.

Laurie Plater, Sunil Bhandari, Anthony Bonadie
and Liora Jacobson of Bhandari & Plater Inc.
for their design excellence.

Heinz Koller of the University of Waterloo
School of Architecture for constructing the
model of the Bibliotheca Alexandrina.

David Takacs, a graduate student of the University
of Waterloo School of Architecture, for his work
on the drawings and the model of Library of a Poet.

The City of Cambridge Archives.

A special thank you to all of the architects, artists,
writers and photographers who generously
contributed their time and work to this project.

Cathi Bond for her love and support, and for
being a constant sounding board.

Special funding for *Logotopia: The Library in Architecture, Art and the Imagination* provided by the Promotion of Architecture Program of the Canada Council for the Arts